Socrates Meets Marx

Other Works of Peter Kreeft from St. Augustine's Press

Philosophy 101 by Socrates
Socrates Meets Descartes
Socrates Meets Freud
Socrates Meets Hume
Socrates Meets Kant
Socrates Meets Kierkegaard
Socrates Meets Machiavelli
Socrates Meets Sartre
The Philosophy of Jesus
Jesus-Shock
Summa Philosophica
Socratic Logic
Socrates' Children: Ancient
Socrates' Children: Medieval
Socrates' Children: Modern
Socrates' Children: Contemporary
Socrates' Children [all four books in one]
An Ocean Full of Angels
The Sea Within
I Surf, Therefore I Am
If Einstein Had Been a Surfer

Socrates Meets Marx

The Father of Philosophy Cross-Examines
the Founder of Communism

A Socratic Dialogue on *The Communist Manifesto*

By Peter Kreeft

ST. AUGUSTINE'S PRESS
South Bend, Indiana

ST. AUGUSTINE'S PRESS
www.staugustine.net

Contents

Introduction

This book is one in a series of Socratic explorations of some of the Great Books. Books in this series are intended to be short, clear, and non-technical, thus fully understandable by beginners. They also introduce (or review) the basic questions in the fundamental divisions of philosophy (see the chapter titles): metaphysics, epistemology, anthropology, ethics, logic, and method. They are designed both for classroom use and for educational do-it-yourselfers.

The "Socrates Meets . . ." books can be read and understood completely on their own, but each is best appreciated after reading the little classic it engages in dialogue.

The setting—Socrates and the author of the Great Book meeting in the afterlife—need not deter readers who do not believe there is an afterlife. For although the two characters and their philosophies are historically real, their conversation, of course, is not and requires a "willing suspension of disbelief". There is no reason the skeptic cannot extend this literary belief also to the setting.

1

The "I"

MARX: I . . . I thought I was dying! And now I . . . I . . .

SOCRATES: That is a profound little word, Karl. Do you know what it means?

MARX: I don't know what you're talking about. I know one thing, though: I'm not dead. I can hear you, and I can see you, too. In fact, you are the ugliest-looking doctor I have ever seen.

SOCRATES: I am not a doctor; I am a philosopher.

MARX: You look like Socrates.

SOCRATES: In this case appearance and reality coincide. I am Socrates.

MARX: But why *you*? We have nothing in common, you and I.

SOCRATES: Oh, I think we do. I think we have at least two things in common: we are probably the two ugliest philosophers in history and the most hated—or loved.

MARX: Where in the world are we?

SOCRATES: Nowhere in the world. We are in the next world.

MARX: Nonsense! There is no "next world".

SOCRATES: Ah . . . excuse me, but what do you think this is?

MARX: A dream, of course. It must be a dream. It certainly can't be real.

SOCRATES: Then who do you think is dreaming the dream?

MARX: My brain matter.

SOCRATES: "My" brain matter, you say? Who is this self that possesses brain matter?

MARX: It is I, Karl Marx, you idiot!

SOCRATES: But what is the meaning of that word you just used, that little word that we all use so easily, the word "I"?

MARX: It's certainly not the soul, as *you* thought it was, "Socrates", or whoever you are.

SOCRATES: Tell me more. If you could teach me where I was wrong, I would be eternally grateful to you.

MARX: Your so-called "soul" is a ghost, a myth, an illusion. There *are* no souls. To be is to be material. It is you, Socrates, who almost single-handedly polluted the waters of philosophy with that muddy myth of the soul, that distraction from everything real, that ghost that you said was haunting the machine of our bodies. I will allow no spooks in my philosophy. I exorcise your ghost. Out, out, damned spirit!

SOCRATES: Alas, it seems that we cannot have the conversation we are destined to have until you are first convinced of an exceedingly elementary point:

that you exist, that there is a self somewhere holding all those body parts together.

MARX: And how do you propose to argue for the existence of this "self"?

SOCRATES: Well, perhaps a modern argument would work for you better than an ancient one. What do you say about Descartes' famous argument, "I think, therefore I am"?

MARX: I say it is a ridiculous argument.

SOCRATES: Why?

MARX: Only an idealist like him, or you, would resort to *thought* to ground real existence. It is the other way round: real existence grounds thought.

SOCRATES: Oh, I quite agree, if by "ground" you mean "cause". Only a thing that exists can think. And thinking does not cause existence.

MARX: You confuse me by agreeing with me.

SOCRATES: Then I will unconfuse you by disagreeing with you. I think our disagreement is not about what *causes* what, but about what *proves* what. I suspect you do not agree that abstract, rational thought (like Descartes' argument) can prove anything real.

MARX: You are right there. I accept only empirical, scientific evidence as proof for anything real.

SOCRATES: And do you have empirical, scientific proof for *that* principle?

MARX: I will not be distracted by your abstract logic. That's why I am suspicious of most of the arguments of you philosophers. Descartes' "I think, therefore I am" is wholly abstract. Nothing concrete proves it or refutes it.

SOCRATES: So you say that the thinking self that Descartes claims to prove is not a reality?

MARX: Exactly.

SOCRATES: What is it, then?

MARX: A dream.

SOCRATES: If the self is a dream, who is the dreamer?

MARX: Brain matter, of course. I prefer "I pass wind, therefore I am" to "I think, therefore I am."

SOCRATES: So smelling is better proof than thinking?

MARX: Indeed it is! It's empirical and, therefore, scientific.

SOCRATES: So you know that you are real, not by thinking, but by sensing?

MARX: Right.

SOCRATES: And is that also the way you know someone else is real, like me?

MARX: It is.

SOCRATES: So you know others in the same way you know yourself: by sensation.

MARX: Correct.

SOCRATES: Do you know my thoughts now? Even before I speak them?

MARX: No.

SOCRATES: Do you know your own thoughts now, before you speak them?

MARX: Of course.

SOCRATES: Why? If you know others in the same way you know yourself, why should there be this great difference?

MARX: What a simplistic question!

SOCRATES: Perhaps it is. But do you have a simplistic answer for me?

MARX: Yes! It is because the chunks of matter that constitute your brain and the chunks of matter that constitute my brain are different and separate in space and do not touch.

SOCRATES: But then why . . .

MARX: Wait! Why am I arguing abstract philosophy with you? What am I doing here? I was in bed waiting to die, and now I am arguing philosophy with Socrates in a dream. This is ridiculous.

SOCRATES: It is not. It is what you must do, what all must do, eventually. It is the first commandment: "Know thyself." It is not an option but a requirement. And while you could easily divert yourself from that task in the other world, that is not permitted here. That is why I have been sent to teach you. In the other world you could easily avoid me—that is, the task I represent, "know thyself." In this world you do not have that option.

MARX: Well, I will play your game, then, simply because I seem to have no other option. Tell me, please, more about this so-called next world. Do you know the future here? The future of life on earth, I mean.

SOCRATES: Yes, some of it, as much as is needed.

MARX: How?

SOCRATES: You are not ready to learn that yet. That would be a diversion and a distraction.

MARX: A diversion from what? What must I do?

SOCRATES: You must remember . . .

MARX: I do not like to remember, I prefer to plan. I prefer the future to the past.

SOCRATES: In other words, you prefer dreams to facts.

MARX: No, no. I am a lover of facts. I am a scientist. In fact, I was the first to find the scientific formula for all of human history. And I found countless facts to prove my formula. You see, Socrates, that is how a scientist proves his ideas: with concrete facts, not with abstract arguments, like you philosophers.

SOCRATES: Our task here is to examine your **"formula for all of human history"**, and the evidence for it in your most famous book, which changed the world.

MARX: You did say "changed the world", didn't you?

SOCRATES: Yes. You, Karl, made a greater difference to historical events, and to the lives of more people, than any other human being in modern history.

MARX: I knew it! I knew it! I succeeded. But I never finished my great book.

SOCRATES: I was not speaking of that overlong, colossal bore *Capital*. I was speaking of *The Communist Manifesto*.

MARX: My rhetorical masterpiece! I knew it was destined to change the face of the earth. What do you want to examine about it?

SOCRATES: Oh, just one little thing: Is it true?

MARX: True? Of course it's true! It changed the world, didn't it? Didn't you say that? It succeeded.

SOCRATES: So the proof of truth is success?

MARX: Certainly.

SOCRATES: Couldn't a lie be successful, if the liar persuaded others to believe it and if he had his way and his will with them? Couldn't a lie change the world, too, if people believed it?

MARX: Not in the long run. History is the womb of truth.

SOCRATES: And just what do you mean by that image?

MARX: That truth is tested by action, not by contemplation or abstract thought or even argument.

SOCRATES: So arguments don't really ever prove anything to be true?

MARX: No, they do not.

SOCRATES: I know you will not produce an argument to prove *that*, then. But would you *explain* it, at least, even though you refuse to prove it?

MARX: The substantive point is this, Socrates: Thinking is itself a concrete act that takes place in history and has material causes. It is not some ghost outside the act, looking at it from some transcendent point of view outside time and space, as you idealists think. That was the fundamental error that you started, Socrates, the error of idealism. And then it was picked up by Plato and Aristotle and Augustine and Aquinas and Descartes and Hegel and their deceived disciples. Too bad I wasn't around in your day, Socrates; I would have stopped that error, which vitiated philosophy for two thousand years. I would have done for you what I did for Hegel: turned you right side up. And turned all of philosophy right side up.

SOCRATES: And what do you mean by *that* image? What is "right-side-up" philosophy and what is "wrong-side-up" philosophy? What was my error, and the error of all those other philosophers, in a word?

MARX: In a word, as I said in my *Theses on Feuerbach*, **"Philosophers have only interpreted the world; the thing is to change it."**

And I could change this world, too, whatever it is and wherever it is, even if it is a dream, as I suppose. For even dreams have to borrow what truth they have from the world, from the only world there is. Hmmm . . . Tell me something about this world. You have workers and employers here, I suppose? You certainly need economists, and . . .

SOCRATES: No. We have no workers or employers, and we need no economists, because we have no money. Your work is over.

MARX: That is impossible. Even a dream should make more sense than that.

SOCRATES: Perhaps you could try to show me why we need economists here.

MARX: I will refute you by your own kind of logic, Socrates. Since I can see you, you must be a bodily being. If you are a bodily being, you must have bodily needs. If you have bodily needs, these must have relative values. It they have relative values, they can be exchanged or bought and sold. If they are exchanged, bought and sold, you need economists, for economics is the science of these things. For instance, that white tunic you are wearing—who made it? Where did you buy it?

SOCRATES: Oh, dear. Must we go into all that before we can explore your book?

MARX: My book is *about* that! Here, let me see that tunic you are wearing. Take it off for me for a minute, please.

SOCRATES: It does not come off. It is not the kind of clothing you know. It does not disguise me, but it reveals me. This is the land of light and of revealing, not of concealing. See, even your own filthy clothes do not come off, no matter how you tug at them. They reveal the soul that wears the body that wears them.

MARX: Ach! What a twisted dream this is! Help!

SOCRATES: That is precisely my purpose here: to help, or at least to begin to help you "untwist" some of the twisted dreams you had and still have. But you are not dreaming now, Karl, you are waking. In fact, you are more awake than you ever were before.

MARX: Then away with it! I do not accept this universe! I will destroy it!

SOCRATES: You no longer have the power to destroy anything here except illusions.

MARX: I shall organize a party! I will find your victims. Whom else are you oppressing, you tyrant of thoughts? I will unite your victims, and we will throw off our chains. I will issue my manifesto: Workers of the Dream World, Unite! You have nothing to lose but your chains! You have a world to win!

SOCRATES: There is no need to shout. No one can hear you but me.

MARX: Then join me, Socrates, and together we shall begin a revolution.

SOCRATES: You don't understand. There is absolutely no need here that could possibly be addressed by your revolution.

MARX: Conservative! Reactionary! Counterrevolutionary! Antidisestablishmentarian!

SOCRATES: Are you finished?

MARX: No!

SOCRATES: I am patient.

MARX: And I am not. I am not patient but agent. What do you think this is, a hospital for minds, with me as the patient and you as the doctor?

SOCRATES: You have said it.

MARX: This is intolerable! This is Hell!

SOCRATES: No, it is only purgatory—purgatory for you and Heaven for me, at the same time. A very economical arrangement, eh?

MARX: What torture will you perform on me, Doctor Socrates? Will you dissect me?

SOCRATES: No, I will dissect only your book.

MARX: Don't you know already exactly what is in my book?

SOCRATES: I do. But *you* may not.

MARX: How can I not know what I wrote myself? If I wrote it, I know it.

SOCRATES: Most of you don't really understand what you write. That is why you need something like me, something like a mirror. I am sent here to be your mirror. Not yet for your soul—that will come later—but for your book. A modest beginning, really.

MARX: I see you have a copy of it in your hand. And so do I! How did they get here? Are there bookstores?

SOCRATES: Another distracting question. I will not answer it.

MARX: Well, if my book remains in the next world, it is truly immortal. What must I do with it?

SOCRATES: It must move from your hand to your head.

2

The Comprehensive
Claim of Marxism

SOCRATES: Perhaps it would be best for you to introduce your book first, to explain its context and its purpose, as if you were teaching it in a university classroom. I think you are much readier to lecture than to dialogue at this point, so perhaps this method would relieve that itch a bit.

MARX: Do you really expect me to respond to an insulting invitation like that?

SOCRATES: Yes.

MARX: Why?

SOCRATES: Because you are an egotist. And also because you have no choice: there is nothing else to do here.

MARX: Hmph! Well, I will take up your challenge.

The book we are about to explore is very short: a pamphlet of only 12,000 words. Yet it has changed the world, as I knew it would. It contains the essentials of Communism in these few pages. All the rest of my writing consists in additions or refinements to this.

I wrote it at age twenty-nine. Engels did not write a word of it. However, he supplied some of the ideas. The *Manifesto* corresponds to the first twenty-five questions in his *Catechism*. More importantly, he supplied most of the money to print it.

It is a Great Book because it finally solves the mystery of man and lays bare the most fundamental laws that have always governed human behavior. I did for man's history what Darwin did for the history of animal species and Newton did for the inorganic universe. It is the supreme achievement of human thought. I was the first to make history truly scientific.

All the philosophers, from Plato on, sought the "philosopher's stone", the world system, the formula. Each claimed to find it, but none did. Every time thought came to a halt before the timeless formula of some philosopher, the world moved on and refuted it.

Then came Hegel, who made change itself the formula. That was true, but not original: Heraclitus, even before your time, Socrates, had seen that "everything flows", like a river. He sought for the *logos*, the law or formula, for universal change; but it was not found until Hegel, who saw for the first time that logic itself moves with history, that truth itself changes according to the pattern of what he called the "dialectic": a *thesis* generates its own *antithesis*, and from this perpetual conflict emerges a *synthesis*, which then becomes a new thesis generating its own new antithesis, and so on until the final synthesis. Hegel, with unbelievable stupidity, identified this with "God", or "The Absolute" or "Spirit"—probably the three worst words in human speech and the three most harmful myths in human thought.

Heraclitus discovered the universality of change, or "becoming". Hegel discovered the logical form of it, the "dialectic". But I discovered its true content: matter, not spirit. Hegel thought that *ideas* caused historical conflicts; I found the causes in the real world. Ideas are only the echo or the effect.

Furthermore, within the real world I found the source of historical change, not in unpredictable individual characters or choices or passions, but in economic determinism. This was the key to making history a science: something predictable and controllable.

The forces of the dialectic of history are economic classes. Class conflict is history's engine.

I was also the first to show how the socialist, classless Utopia of which others had dreamed would grow like a flower from the plant of my present world. For once the number of classes is reduced to one—the proletariat—conflict is reduced to zero.

This is accomplished by the elimination of the only other remaining class, the bourgeoisie. The meaning of my era is precisely there: Capitalism had already reduced the plethora of classes that had characterized feudalism to just two, the bourgeoisie and the proletariat. The Communist revolution will be the last great event in history, for it will eliminate the bourgeoisie, leaving only **"the dictatorship of the proletariat"**, as I said in my *Critique of the Gotha Program* and elsewhere, that is, a society of perfect equality and justice, where **"the free development of each is the condition for the free development of all"**, and where, as I said in the same book, all things flow **"from each according to his ability to each according to his need."**

SOCRATES: That was a wonderful speech, Karl! It did exactly what it needed to do, in introducing your book. It was admirably clear and simple: even I could understand it. It was powerful and appealing: you are truly a great rhetorician. Lastly, and best of all, it was short.

MARX: So if you are satisfied, let us *do* it, not just think about it. Will you join the Party?

SOCRATES: Well, now, I think you will find some difficulty in organizing that kind of thing here.

MARX: I am not afraid of any challenge, even in my dreams.

SOCRATES: You don't understand.

MARX: What is the problem?

SOCRATES: Well, in addition to the little detail that we are not in your dream but quite real, we have one other little thing that we have to take care of before we can think about practicing your philosophy.

MARX: What is that?

SOCRATES: What do you think? What should you make sure of first, before you put any philosophy into practice?

MARX: That I have the money needed. Is Engels here, too?

SOCRATES: No, something more basic than that.

MARX: There is nothing more basic than that.

SOCRATES: Yes, there is.

MARX: That I have the power base? Fear not; I shall create it.

SOCRATES: No, something else.

MARX: Associates? Organizational skills?

SOCRATES: Something about the philosophy rather than about you. What do you want to be sure a philosophy is?

MARX: Dynamic? Radical? Progressive? No? You still shake your bulbous, ugly head! Challenging, engaging, galvanizing to action? No? Flattering, perhaps? Sly and clever and winsome? No? Original? Creative? Interesting? No, still! Surely you are not suggesting that it be comfortably traditional? No, again. What, then? I give up this demeaning guessing game. What are you after? Tell me the secret. What is the occult quality that you demand in a philosophy before you will put it into practice?

SOCRATES: I was thinking of *truth*.

MARX: Oh.

SOCRATES: Is that your only reply? That one little syllable?

MARX: But practice will reveal that, Socrates. Truth always emerges, eventually, from the process of history, the dialectic. Truth does not come outside of action and before it; it comes *in* action and as the result of action.

SOCRATES: Is that so?

MARX: It is so, I assure you.

SOCRATES: So it is *true* that truth only emerges from the process?

MARX: Yes.

SOCRATES: And are we in the process now, or are we outside it and at its end?

MARX: We are in process.

SOCRATES: And truth is not *before* this process, or *outside* it, but only emerges from it?

MARX: That is what I said. You have a very short memory.

SOCRATES: Then, since we are only in the process and not outside it, how can we know what is outside the process?

MARX: We can't.

SOCRATES: We are like fish, then, in the sea, who cannot fly above the sea like birds.

MARX: Right.

SOCRATES: So we cannot know what is or is not outside the process, just as a fish cannot know what is or is not outside the sea?

MARX: Right again. You are beginning to understand my point, Socrates.

SOCRATES: Then how can you know that there is no truth outside the process?

MARX: What? What's that you say?

SOCRATES: If fish cannot know what is outside the sea, they cannot know what is *not* outside the sea, either. So if we cannot know any truth outside time, we cannot know that there *is* no such thing as truth outside time, either. But you said you did know precisely that: that there is no truth outside time.

MARX: I will not let myself be tricked by some philosopher's abstract logical argument and diverted from the real into the ideal. All your own ideas, Socrates, including that static logic of yours, too, are nothing but the product of your pre-industrial peasant-aristocrat-conservative social order.

SOCRATES: And yours?

MARX: All ideas are the products of social conditions.

SOCRATES: But your social conditions, including your education, were thoroughly bourgeois. If ideas are nothing but products of their social order, your Communism must be a thoroughly bourgeois idea.

MARX: I need not answer your pitiful logic, Socrates. It is impotent. You seek in vain to slay the juggernaut of history's dialectic with the weapons of words. Words are mere shadows, spectres, ghosts.

SOCRATES: Including your words, Karl? Are they also spectres?

MARX: You keep doing that, Socrates! It is a most annoying habit.

SOCRATES: Isn't that image—that of a spectre—exactly the one you used for your own words, or your own ideas, namely, Communism, in the very first line of your book? Here it is: **"A spectre is haunting Europe—the spectre of Communism."**

MARX: I must warn you, Socrates, that your habit of throwing other people's words back at them will not win you many friends. It will only win arguments.

SOCRATES: My purpose here is not to win friends, or to win arguments, either, but to be your helper, if not your friend, by being a mirror held up to your mind so that you may know yourself.

MARX: Are you so naïve as to expect me to believe you are my helper when you subject me to such torture? And to expect me to accept it as in my own best interests?

SOCRATES: Yes, indeed. Unless you want to be a comic figure instead of a serious one. For I can think of nothing more comic than a philosophy that does not account for its own creator. A philosophy without a philosopher—now that's a paradox.

MARX: Is your task here to dissect me or my book?

SOCRATES: Only your book, for now. But that task is a means to the higher end of knowing yourself. Are you ready to begin?

MARX: Go ahead, do your worst, Socrates!

SOCRATES: No, Karl, I will obey my mother instead of you: she always told me to do my best.

3

The Beginning:
Is All History Oppression?

SOCRATES: We have already quoted your famous beginning—

MARX: That is the beginning only of the preface, not of the book. The key sentence in the book is the first one *after* the preface, in chapter 1: **"The history of all hitherto existing society is the history of class struggles."** Everything follows from that.

SOCRATES: Yes. But the *reader* begins with the preface. So let us explore that first. You say:

> A spectre is haunting Europe—the spectre of Communism. All the Powers of old Europe have entered into a holy alliance to exorcize this spectre: Pope and Czar, Metternich and Guizot, French Radicals and German police spies. . . . Communism is already acknowledged by all European Powers to be itself a Power.

MARX: Well?

SOCRATES: Well, I warned you I was going to ask the simple little question, the child's question, "But is it *true*?" In truth, when you wrote these words there were exactly two Communists in Europe: you and Engels.

MARX: A minor technicality.

SOCRATES: And the next point, too, which explains the title "Manifesto", is simply a bald-faced lie:

It is high time that Communists should openly, in the face of the whole world, publish their views, their aims, their tendencies, and meet this nursery tale of the Spectre of Communism with a Manifesto of the party itself. To this end, Communists of various nationalities have assembled in London, and sketched the following Manifesto.

There was no such thing as the Communist Party anywhere on earth when you wrote this, except perhaps in that ideal world, that world of ideas, of which you always speak so disparagingly. Nor did anyone "assemble" in London to produce this *Manifesto*; it was your own solitary work.

MARX: How do you know all that?

SOCRATES: I will not tell you. It is enough that you know that I know.

MARX: Then perhaps you also know what my response will be to a philosopher like you who accuses me of not conforming to some abstract, timeless "truth" that is already "there", like the stars, and can only be contemplated. I value action over contemplation. I say that the highest truth is the historical future. And my words bring about that future. My words *produce* truth instead of passively reflecting it. Every word of this book must be interpreted and understood in that light and evaluated by that standard; every word is calculated to bring about an effect, to create a new truth on earth. My book called into existence the truths it uttered. It *created* Communism.

SOCRATES: Do you say, then, that any lie I might tell becomes true when it succeeds in deceiving people?

MARX: No, no, that is not what I mean.

SOCRATES: What *do* you mean, then? Let us try to find out by a thought experiment. You do not believe any God really exists, do you?

MARX: No. God is a myth, a dream, a drug.

SOCRATES: Well, then, suppose that I were to write a "God Manifesto" asserting the reality of God, and suppose I convinced half the people on earth to believe it. Would you say, then, that I created God as a new truth? Suppose I compounded the lie by claiming that I am God, the Creator, and that I have incarnated myself as a creature. Suppose I get half the world to worship me, thus becoming the most influential man in history. Have I then succeeded in making the myth true, by your standards? Have I not then called into existence Christianity, just as you called into existence Communism? Why is one truer than the other? In fact, why isn't Christianity more true, since it is more powerful, more successful, more active, more world-changing? By your standard of truth, you should be a Christian!

MARX: Impossibility! Idiocy! Horse-droppings!

SOCRATES: Are those new logical refutations I have not heard of?

MARX: You misunderstand me. I do not say that mind can call truth into existence. I am not an idealist philosopher; I am a scientist. I say that truth is correspondence with objective reality. Truth is objective.

SOCRATES: Oh! Then you do not agree with those disciples of yours who say that truth is only the hypocritical mask on the face of political power?

MARX: Certainly not. Who are these people? They are certainly not disciples of mine. I say that truth is objective.

SOCRATES: Good. Then we can continue to investigate whether the statements in your book are true, since we have agreed about the meaning of truth. That is progress greater than many philosophers could make.

Let us begin by investigating your first sentence, which is your formula for all of human history: **"The history of all hitherto existing society is the history of class struggles."**

MARX: What do you want to investigate about it?

SOCRATES: Why, whether it is true! "True" in the simple, ordinary sense of "true" that we just agreed on, rather than in the sense you used a few minutes ago when you said that your *Manifesto* "created" the truth of Communism.

MARX: I was not wrong in saying that. If the book created Communism, then it created the fact that Communism existed, so that the assertion that "Communism exists" was not true before my book was written, but it was true after it. In that way, it did create the truth of Communism, as birth creates the truth of a new baby.

SOCRATES: I understand. And so the New Testament, or the Church, "created the truth" of Christianity, too, in the same way, then. Is that what you say?

MARX: Created its existence, yes.

SOCRATES: But you do not believe that what the Bible says, or what the Church says, is true.

MARX: Right. I do not.

SOCRATES: But what Communism says *is* true, you say.

MARX: Yes.

SOCRATES: Then we must test this claim that is the historical foundation of Communism: Is it true that all history is class conflict? For this is your "Archimedean point". As you know, Archimedes said, "Give me only a lever and a fulcrum to rest it on, and I can move the world." And here is your first point, your premise, your fulcrum for the lever of Communism with which you will move the whole world. I see you nodding your agreement. Well, you understand, then, that this is why we must first investigate whether it is true that all history is class conflict.

MARX: Yes. And it *is* true. For instance—

SOCRATES: No, please do not multiply instances. I know that many exist. What we need to know is whether any counter-instances exist.

MARX: Why do you insist on that?

SOCRATES: You say that *all* history is class conflict. We do not prove that by showing that *some* history is class conflict. But we would *dis*prove it if we showed that some history is *not* class conflict. In logical terms, a universal affirmative proposition is not proved by a particular affirmative proposition, but it is disproved by a particular negative proposition.

MARX: I understand the rules of logic.

SOCRATES: But surely we can find exactly that disproof? Surely classes have sometimes cooperated—for instance, against foreign enemies or for religious purposes. And surely most people throughout history have just gone on about their daily lives, their families, their pleasures and pains, their births and deaths, without ever a thought about the class struggle.

MARX: I have two answers, Socrates. The first is that I am speaking only about all known history, all recorded history. There may have been some primitive communist societies that we do not know of.

SOCRATES: Actually, Engels made that point in a footnote to a later edition of your *Manifesto*. But the claim is still enormous, even with this qualification.

MARX: My second answer is that the lack of awareness of class conflict does not prove its nonexistence. A thing can exist when you are not conscious of it. Truth is objective, remember.

SOCRATES: A very good point, Karl. Surely some distant planet, or some hidden chemical element, could exist without anyone being aware of it. But how could **"class conflict"** exist if no one felt it? What could *class struggle* possibly mean in a society in which all, even the lower classes, accepted the class system, one in which few or none *felt* oppressed or wanted to overthrow their superiors, or even wanted to climb up into a superior class? And many societies in the past seem to have been like that. What could **"class conflict"** mean in such a society?

MARX: I do not accept your assumption that many societies have been like that. But even if such societies existed, they could still contain class conflict but their consciousness had not yet been enlightened to it. They were oppressed but too stupid to realize it.

SOCRATES: Then how were they oppressed, if they were happy? Where does **"class conflict"** exist when it is felt by no one? Would not that be an oxymoron, like war among pacifists, or hunger among the satiated?

MARX: Read my next sentence, Socrates. That answers your question; that tells you where the class conflict is: it is between the classes, not necessarily in the minds or feelings of individuals who make up the classes. I write:

> **Freeman and slave, patrician and plebeian, lord and serf, guild-master and journeyman, . . . stood in constant opposition to one another, carried on an uninterrupted, now hidden, now open fight, a fight that each time ended, either in a revolutionary reconstitution of society at large, or in the common ruin of the contending classes.**

SOCRATES: Do you really believe that all of human history is as dismal as that? That it is *nothing* but oppression, **"constant"** and **"uninterrupted"**?

MARX: Yes, indeed.

SOCRATES: So when the guild-master and the journeyman, for instance, or the master-craftsman and
the apprentice, freely joined with each other by a mutual contract for the profit and satisfaction of both,
that relationship was in fact really oppression even
though both experienced it as cooperation?

MARX: Yes! For the oppression is structural, not necessarily psychological. It exists in the very structure
of the economic classes, even when it is not felt in the
minds and desires of individuals.

SOCRATES: But how could such a massive and harmful thing as this—essentially universal slavery—not
register on people's consciousness? How could slaves
be happy in their slavery? Is that not contrary to human nature?

MARX: I do not believe there is such a thing as a universal and unchangeable "human nature". Human
nature is created by social conditions and changed
by social conditions. It is a radically different nature
in one society from what it is in another.

SOCRATES: Do you think people can be happy when
they are oppressed? That slaves can be happy in their
slavery?

MARX: No, I do not think that.

SOCRATES: And do you say that the apprentice was
oppressed or enslaved by the master?

MARX: Yes.

SOCRATES: Then he cannot have been happy.

MARX: I do not think he *was* happy. Only one could
be the master, but all would have liked to be. Surely

the apprentice would rather have been the master, would have liked to displace the master. But he could not, or not yet. Surely that is the only reason he endured his shackles and served the master: out of self-interest, biding his time. Surely you do not think this was from *charity* rather than self-interest?

SOCRATES: Hmmm—your view of human nature and human relationships sounds quite similar to that of another philosopher I cross-examined a short time ago, Nicolo Machiavelli. Well, I do not believe that men act out of charity all the time, or even most of the time; but you seem to believe that they do this none of the time. But let us suppose you are right: let us suppose that the apprentice and the master are both motivated by self-interest and nothing but self-interest, without even a spark of friendship or loyalty or affection or respect or duty—still, the very structure of the relationship seems designed to fulfill the self-interest of both, not just one, for the apprentice needs the master's expertise, and the master needs the apprentice's work. You said that even if the people did not feel oppressed, the structures were oppressive. But the structure seems to be cooperative rather than oppressive. So we have found this "constant" and "uninterrupted" oppression neither in the people nor in the structures.

MARX: Do you believe, Socrates, that the relationship between a rich man and a prostitute is cooperative rather than oppressive because the rich man *needs* the services of the prostitute and she *needs* his money?

SOCRATES: Good for you, Karl! You are responding logically. No, I do not say that. But don't *you* say that? Don't you say that the guild-master is only a craft-prostitute and that the teacher is simply an intellectual prostitute?

MARX: Yes—except under Communism. You see, I have not only the diagnosis but also the cure. Just as a disease is cured only by finding its cause and then removing it, so the only way to end oppression is to remove its cause, which is the class system.

SOCRATES: You do not believe that oppression is caused by oppressors, then? By wicked individuals and wicked choices?

MARX: No. They are only the instruments of the social system, the class system. That is why oppression can be ended, not by appeals to virtue and preachings against wickedness, but only by destroying the class system, and doing so without replacing it with another one. And that can be done only by Communism.

SOCRATES: That is a bold claim.

MARX: It is.

SOCRATES: Before we go on to look at the next major point in your book, I would like to understand what kind of claim you are making. What I mean is: Should I look at Communism as something like a religion or something like science?

MARX: It is completely non-religious and completely scientific.

SOCRATES: Let me see whether we understand each other. By "scientific", do you mean "empirical" or something else?

MARX: Empirical, of course. What could "something else" be?

SOCRATES: Well, some claim that theology is a science, although it is not empirical, because it uses logical demonstrations.

MARX: No, no, a science must be empirical and nothing but empirical.

SOCRATES: Let us be more detailed about this. Do you say that all of a science's evidence and verification and proofs must also be empirical?

MARX: Yes. Otherwise it is not really a science.

SOCRATES: And do you say that in order to refute a scientific claim you must also use empirical evidence, just as you must use empirical evidence to prove the claim?

MARX: Certainly.

SOCRATES: So if someone made a religious claim—for instance, that an all-powerful, all-knowing, and all-loving God had created you and was at this moment providentially taking perfect care of your life—would you say it would be correct to call that claim unscientific?

MARX: Indeed.

SOCRATES: Let me see whether your reason for saying this is the same as mine. I would say that this claim about divine providence, whether it is true or false, is *unscientific* because the believer in divine providence could not answer the following question: "Tell me, O believer, how could this belief of yours ever possibly be disproved? For instance, if two good, innocent friends of yours died suddenly in a tragic accident, would that empirical fact refute your belief in your God and in his providence?" I think the believer would reply "No", don't you?

MARX: Yes.

SOCRATES: And if I persisted in my questioning and asked the believer whether ten or a hundred or a thousand such events would disprove his belief, do you think he would reply "Yes" then?

MARX: No, he would say "No".

SOCRATES: Finally, if I asked him *how many* such bad events would disprove his belief in a good God, would he give me a number?

MARX: No. He could not give you a number.

SOCRATES: And if I were to ask him to describe anything at all that we could see in this world that would prove to him that the good God he believed in was an unreal myth, what do you think he would reply?

MARX: He would be unable to give you what you demanded.

SOCRATES: And so, would I be right to conclude that his belief is not scientific?

MARX: Indeed you would.

SOCRATES: And is it for this reason: that it is not possible, in principle, even in the imagination, to disprove it empirically?

MARX: Yes. It is a religious belief, and not rational.

SOCRATES: Well, it is not *scientific*, at any rate. Whether or not all that is not scientific, that is, not empirically verifiable or falsifiable, is for that reason *irrational* is a question we have not yet investigated, and we may come back to it later. But we do not need to assume that all that is not scientific is not rational—an assumption many would disagree with. All we need to do in order to show that a belief is not scientific is to show that the believer would not allow any empirically observable state of affairs to disprove it.

MARX: I agree. If it is not empirically falsifiable in principle, then it is not scientific, but religious or quasi-religious.

SOCRATES: Let us now apply this principle to the sentence that you say is the key sentence in your book, the first one, the one from which everything else flows: **"The history of all hitherto existing society is the history of class struggles."** You explain in the next sentence that this means that all social relationships are relationships of oppression: **"freeman and slave, patrician and plebeian, lord and serf, guild-master and journeyman, . . . stood in constant opposition to one another, carried on an uninterrupted, now hidden, now open fight."**

MARX: And I stand by that.

SOCRATES: When I first quoted this sentence, I expressed surprise at your belief that all human history was nothing but oppression, and I presented an example of a social relationship—that of apprentice and guild-master—that seemed to refute it by being a relationship of mutual cooperation rather than oppression. But you interpreted that relationship as a relationship of oppression, too. And you did the same with the relationship between teacher and student. So now I ask you whether you can tell me what social relationship could possibly be *non*-oppressive. What relationship could anyone find, anywhere, that would disprove your first sentence?

MARX: I can answer that question easily, Socrates. The relationships of equality that characterize a Communist society are all non-oppressive relationships.

SOCRATES: But a Communist society has not yet existed at any time in history before your time, has it?

MARX: Not yet.

SOCRATES: But your statement—the one we are investigating—is about history, about the past, not about the future. What might we search for in history that would disprove your statement? Can you describe what would empirically falsify your belief? Suppose we could visit every society that has ever existed. Would we find any example of a society that was non-oppressive and yet was not a Communist society?

MARX: We would not.

SOCRATES: Is this true because we would observe it to be so, or because we have defined it to be so even before we begin to observe?

MARX: What do you mean by that question?

SOCRATES: I mean: Can you imagine it not being true? Can you write a fantasy about a world in which it is not true? Like a world in which men have two heads? Or would it be literally unimaginable, like a world in which men are not men?

MARX: I suppose one could imagine such a world, but it would be a pure fantasy.

SOCRATES: Then please tell me what such a society would look like—one in which there was no oppression and yet no Communism.

MARX: I cannot do that. It is impossible.

SOCRATES: Then it seems that you have simply defined "oppressive" as "non Communist" and "non-oppressive" as "Communist."

MARX: No, it is a matter of empirical truth, not a matter of arbitrary word use.

SOCRATES: I wonder. Let me try again to test you on this point. Can you imagine the possibility of some historian discovering some Communist society in the past, or on some remote island?

MARX: Certainly.

SOCRATES: And such a society would necessarily be non-oppressive?

MARX: Yes.

SOCRATES: Why?

MARX: Why, because it was Communist, of course.

SOCRATES: Would there be any other reason?

MARX: No.

SOCRATES: And all the other societies that we would ever discover in the past or in some remote place in the present—they would be oppressive if they were not Communist societies too?

MARX: Yes.

SOCRATES: Simply because they were not Communist?

MARX: Yes.

SOCRATES: And all societies that we might create in the future, if they were not Communist societies, would they be oppressive too?

MARX: Yes.

SOCRATES: Necessarily so?

MARX: Yes.

SOCRATES: Simply because they were not Communist?

MARX: Yes.

SOCRATES: Then it seems that you are simply using these two sets of words interchangeably, and that you do not mean anything more by "oppressive" than "not Communist."

MARX: That is not true.

SOCRATES: Then please tell me what you mean by an "oppressive" society. Is it perhaps one that removes people's natural rights?

MARX: No, I do not believe in universal, unchangeable "natural rights."

SOCRATES: What about a society that murders its citizens simply because they do not believe in the political philosophy of those in power? Or one that steals the property of its citizens? Or one which makes its citizens unhappy, so that they must be forbidden to travel and leave the country, and must be kept in check by a large and powerful police force that rules by terror? Or simply one that does something—anything—to its citizens that they consider oppressive? Would you accept any of these things as being sure marks of an oppressive society? For that is what most people would mean by the term.

MARX: What if I say yes?

SOCRATES: Then I will use your answer to judge most Communist societies in history as very oppressive indeed, and much more so than most non-Communist ones.

MARX: You are using your own definitions of oppression to judge, then.

SOCRATES: No, I am using yours, if you will accept them.

MARX: I do not accept them!

SOCRATES: Then we are back where we were a moment ago: you cannot specify any meaning to the word "oppression" beyond "non-Communism" You make it true *by definition* that all history before Communism is oppression.

MARX: It is not just an empty tautology. It is true.

SOCRATES: Perhaps it is not just a tautology. And I do not claim to have proved that it is not true. I only claim to have shown that it is not a scientific belief.

MARX: Of course it is scientific. It makes history into a science for the first time.

SOCRATES: So you say. But science is empirical, or *a posteriori*, as the logicians say, while we have just shown that your belief is not; that it is an *a priori*.

MARX: So what does that mean, O great logician?

SOCRATES: By the standards we agreed to a few minutes ago, it means that it is a religious belief, like the belief that there is a good and loving God no matter how much evil we experience in the world.

MARX: Ridiculous! My system is scientific, not religious. It is empirical.

SOCRATES: You have not shown how your belief is empirical. But you have shown something empirical about the belief: that it has turned your face very red.

4

The Present Time:
Can Human Nature Change?

MARX: I am red not because I am embarrassed, Socrates, and unable to answer you. I am red because I am angry at your injustice. Your critique of my philosophy of history so far—or rather, of only the first sentence of it—has not been historical, but only logical. You have used that abstract and timeless logic that you invented, rather than the concrete and moving logic of history that I learned from Hegel. So your critique is as unfair as if you would criticize a dance for not obeying the laws of painting.

SOCRATES: I am pleased that you are beginning to argue logically, Karl, even as you argue against logic. For even bad logic is better than good propaganda. I am also pleased that you appeal to a timeless and universal justice to which you expect both of us to be subject, though your philosophy does not allow the existence of any such justice. Your practice seems to contradict your theory. Perhaps we should pay less attention to your theory and more to your practice. And the same with Communism.

MARX: There is no contradiction. I stand by my theory as well as my practice—and that of Communism as well.

SOCRATES: Well, then, go ahead with your new dialectical logic, and spin out your philosophy of history for me, as a spider's web is spun from its first thread. Your whole philosophy of history stems from the assumption we have just examined and found questionable: that all past history has been nothing but opposition and class conflict. We have examined the first thread of your web, but we have not given you a chance to show us the rest of the web yet.

MARX: Are you making fun of my looks, Socrates, calling me a spider?

SOCRATES: I? Make fun of another man's looks? Look at me, Karl. I assure you, I have been called worse things than "spider". But no, I do not mean to call you names, only to examine your book.

MARX: Then let's do it instead of talking about doing it, O master theorist!

SOCRATES: Touché. Your next point, after summarizing all of past history as oppression, is to summarize the significance of the time that was your present—the nineteenth century—as opportunity. Finally, you prophesy the future as Communism's triumph. Is that a fair summary of your philosophy of history in three sentences?

MARX: As far as it goes, yes.

SOCRATES: So now we must proceed to your second point: the difference between all past eras and your present era. In one word, what do you say it is?

MARX: The bourgeoisie. As I write next, **"In the earlier epochs of history, we find almost everywhere a complicated arrangement of society—"**

SOCRATES: Excuse me for interrupting, but this point seems striking. Almost everyone else, if asked how modern society differs from past societies, would say it is *more* complicated, but you say it is less!

MARX: Yes, I do. And I would appreciate it if you would not interrupt me again, because—

SOCRATES: I cannot promise you that.

MARX: There you go again! How am I expected to—

SOCRATES: Expected by whom? Who do you think is expecting something from you?

MARX: You just interrupted—

SOCRATES: Again. Yes. I am teasing you, Karl. Where is your sense of humor?

MARX: This *Manifesto* is serious!

SOCRATES: Oh, yes, it is indeed—terribly serious. I was hoping to find some things in you that I did not find in your book, such as a sense of humor in your soul.

MARX: You will find in me only flesh and bones and hair and nails and brain and nervous system, but no "soul".

SOCRATES: Hmmm—that is what I am afraid of. But come, no more teasing. Finish reading. I am finished interrupting.

MARX:

In the earlier epochs of history, we find almost everywhere a complicated arrangement of society into various orders, a manifold gradation of social rank. In ancient Rome we have patricians, knights, plebeians, slaves; in

the Middle Ages, feudal lords, vassals, guild-masters, journeymen, apprentices, serfs; in almost all of these classes, again, subordinate gradations.

The modern bourgeois society that has sprouted from the ruins of feudal society has not done away with class antagonisms. It has but established new classes, new conditions of oppression, new forms of struggle in place of the old ones.

Our epoch, the epoch of the bourgeoisie, possesses, however, this distinctive feature: it has simplified the class antagonisms. Society as a whole is more and more splitting up into two great hostile camps, into two great classes directly facing one another: Bourgeoisie and Proletariat.

SOCRATES: Let us consider this point before passing on to the next. It is a more detailed version of your first point, that all of history is the history of class conflict. The words you use for all relationships between classes are the words of war: **"antagonisms"**, **"oppression"**, **"struggle"**, **"hostile camps"**.

MARX: We've argued about that already. My new point here is that the class warfare has changed in quantity. There are now only two armies.

SOCRATES: And to evaluate your new point we need to understand it; and to understand it we need to understand its terms. So please tell me exactly what you mean by these two new terms by which you define the social situation in your time: the **"Bourgeoisie"** and the **"Proletariat"**.

MARX: The bourgeoisie is the class of those who own the means of production.

SOCRATES: Production of what?

MARX: Of social wealth. And under Capitalism these people are the Capitalists, those who have capital—wealth that is over and above what they need for their basic subsistence and survival and which they are free to invest at interest, thus becoming wealthier. In fact, under Capitalism the wealthier one is, the wealthier one can become, and the faster. Thus the rich get richer, and the poor get poorer.

The proletariat, on the other hand, are those who do not own the means of production and who, therefore, in order to survive, must sell themselves as laborers for wages paid to them by the bourgeoisie, the Capitalists. You see, it is the master-slave relationship in economic terms.

SOCRATES: You see the conflict between rich and poor, between the "haves" and the "have-nots", as inevitable, then?

MARX: It is not just rich and poor, that is, those who have wealth and those who do not have it. It is between those who have the power to produce more wealth and those who do not.

SOCRATES: So you focus on power more than simply wealth, and on the control of the future more than on control of the present.

MARX: You could say so. But my main point about my present time was that now there is only one class of "haves" and one of "have nots", so there is no longer class conflict among the "haves" or among "have-nots", but only the one remaining conflict.

And the practical significance of this fact is enormous: For the first time in history, a single worldwide proletarian revolution can abolish the bourgeoisie and thus abolish class conflict, which is the motor of all history.

SOCRATES: So this revolution would really end history!

MARX: Yes.

SOCRATES: What a remarkable claim! That the end of history will happen at some time in history.

MARX: It is not a logical self-contradiction, as it seems to be. It is perfectly logical, if you only look at its material content instead of its abstract form—in other words, if you are scientific, like me, rather than abstractly philosophical, like you. You see, history is change. Without social change, there is no history. And the cause of social change is class conflict. Therefore, without class conflict, there is no history. Remove the cause, and you remove the effect. But class conflict can cease if and only if there are no more classes. And that can happen only when the number of classes falls to two, so that the elimination of one class by the other creates a classless society. And that is the Communist revolution. Therefore history can end only through the historic act of the Communist revolution.

SOCRATES: That is certainly a fascinating story. It remains to be seen whether it is fact or fiction.

MARX: What do you mean, "fact or fiction"?

SOCRATES: Why, whether it is true, of course.

MARX: And how do you propose to find that out?

SOCRATES: Since the end of history has not happened yet, you cannot know whether it is true or false by empirical observation.

MARX: But to say it has not happened yet, to say that it has not been observed yet, does not prove that it is fiction. It *will* be observed, when it happens.

SOCRATES: But we cannot observe the future yet, and therefore we cannot verify or falsify this idea yet.

MARX: And therefore you conclude that this is not a scientific idea?

SOCRATES: No, I do not say that. I say that there is a second way to test an idea, even a scientific idea, in addition to empirical observation.

MARX: Impossible. If it's not empirical, it's not scientific.

SOCRATES: Suppose a scientific theory contained a logical self-contradiction? Would that not prove the theory false?

MARX: Actually, no! Living contradictions are what history is made of. Your logic rejects contradictions because it rejects history. But Hegel's logic, my logic, embraces contradictions. That is what moves the dialectic of history: the contradiction between thesis and antithesis.

SOCRATES: Oh, I am perfectly willing to grant you, for the sake of argument, that Hegel is right about his dialectic, and that you are, too. But that is not *contradiction*, that is *contrariety*.

MARX: What do you mean?

SOCRATES: Hot and cold, good and evil, and visible and invisible are pairs of opposites, or contrary *terms*. These may quite easily coexist; for instance, a man may be both good and evil or both visible (because of his body) and invisible (because of his soul). It is not two *terms*, or two real things designated by two terms, but two *propositions* that can be contradictory. And while two contrary terms may both be there at the same time, like good and evil in the same man, two contradictory propositions cannot both be true at the same time. For instance, although Socrates may be both good and evil at the same time, it cannot be true that Socrates has some goodness and that Socrates does not have some goodness at the same time.

MARX: But Socrates can be both good and evil at the same time. You admit that. You can be that living contradiction.

SOCRATES: No, that is not a contradiction, that is different; that is why we need a different word for it. The traditional word for it in logic is *contrariety*, or *opposites*. You are mistaken to call them contradictions.

MARX: Thank you, inventor of logic, for your lesson in abstract wordplay.

SOCRATES: I will turn it into a lesson in practical, concrete history. Look here—you say that history will end by a Communist revolution. You Communists say that proposition is true, do you not?

MARX: Yes.

SOCRATES: But your opponents, the anti-Communists, say it is false, do they not?

MARX: Yes.

SOCRATES: So Communists and anti-Communists contradict each other. The proposition believed by one must be true, and the proposition believed by the other must be false.

MARX: Of course. I do not contradict the world there.

SOCRATES: What then *do* you contradict the world about? What do you say about history and contradiction that the world does not know?

MARX: That both Communism and anti-Communism are necessary parts of the dialectic, and thus both are true for their place in history. Thus contradictions are both true and necessary.

SOCRATES: Perhaps both are *necessary*, but then one is a necessary truth, and the other a necessary falsehood.

MARX: You could put it like that. But while Capitalism is false from the Communist point of view, it is true from the Capitalist point of view.

SOCRATES: If that is so, then the Capitalist point of view itself is not true, and the Communist point of view is. In other words, Capitalism is false, and Communism is true.

MARX: You seem to be agreeing with me, but I think you are not. I suspect, Socrates, that when you say that "Capitalism is false, and Communism is true", you are thinking of some universal, abstract, timeless, ahistorical truth. That is where we differ: I do not believe in such a truth. I believe truth itself changes through history.

SOCRATES: Do you deny, then, that we can know that a scientific theory is false simply because it contradicts itself logically?

MARX: Give me an example.

SOCRATES: Suppose someone propounds the theory that Julius Caesar was assassinated by Karl Marx. I claim that we can know this is false simply because it contains a self-contradiction, one that we all recognize—which is why we all know that this theory is false.

MARX: What self-contradiction?

SOCRATES: We all know that a living man cannot be assassinated by one who is not living, and we all know that Caesar was assassinated when you were not alive.

MARX: All right, then. I agree that a theory that contradicts itself in that way must be false. But nothing in my theory contradicts itself in that way.

SOCRATES: That is what we must now investigate. For if we find such a contradiction in it, we shall know it is false.

MARX: But you must interpret it correctly. It is very easy to find apparent contradictions.

SOCRATES: Quite so. So we shall have to understand it before we test it. That is why I insist on defining terms before testing propositions by argument.

MARX: Go ahead, then. I'm getting tired of all this empty, abstract, general logic.

SOCRATES: Then here is something full and concrete and specific: I find three things in the passage you just read that seem to contain contradictions. Perhaps they do not; perhaps I have misunderstood them. So you must explain to me what you mean by each one.

MARX: I will be happy to enlighten you, Socrates. If you think you see any contradictions there, I'm sure you do misunderstand.

SOCRATES: We shall see. Here is my first question. You say that conflict can cease *only* when all classes except one are eliminated, correct?

MARX: Yes.

SOCRATES: So there cannot be a conversion or a change of heart or a change in human nature from warlike to peaceful before your revolution?

MARX: There cannot be, and there has not been.

SOCRATES: And in your historical present, your nine-teenth century, you find two classes left, the bourgeoisie and the proletariat, correct?

MARX: Yes.

SOCRATES: And it is the proletariat who will rise and revolt against their oppressors, correct?

MARX: Yes. The bourgeoisie will certainly not rise against the proletariat, because they need the proletariat. But the proletariat do not need the bourgeoisie. It is Hegel's "master-slave dialectic": The master is enslaved to his slave, that is, to his need for his slave. That is why masters never revolt against slaves, but only slaves against masters.

SOCRATES: I see. So in your story the proletariat are the heroes, and the bourgeoisie are the villains.

MARX: Historically speaking, you could say that. But I do not appeal to any timeless truth to make that judgment.

SOCRATES: Do the men of these two classes have two different natures, one good and the other bad?

MARX: No. They cannot help acting as they do.

SOCRATES: If you were to take each member of the bourgeoisie and make him proletarian simply by depriving him of his ownership of the means of production, would he then act like one of the bourgeoisie or like a proletarian?

MARX: Like a proletarian.

SOCRATES: And if you were to take each proletarian and make him a member of the bourgeoisie by giving him ownership of the means of production, would he act like one of the bourgeoisie or like a proletarian?

MARX: Like one of the bourgeoisie.

SOCRATES: So men are not divided into good and evil, selfish and unselfish, but into bourgeoisie and proletariat.

MARX: Yes. Men are all selfish. They act differently only because they are members of different classes.

SOCRATES: I see. Well, then, if all men alike are selfish, and if human nature is not changed by putting men into different social classes, then your Communist revolution will not change human nature, either.

Men will still be selfish and competitive after the revolution just as they were before it. So history will *not* end. Strife will continue.

MARX: No, no, you don't understand, Socrates. Human nature is malleable. If you change the class structure, you change its content, just as if you change the words in a document, you change its meaning. The revolution will produce a new man, one without conflicts and antagonisms. As I said in my *Critique of the Gotha Program*, men will live **"from each according to his ability to each according to his need."** And **"the free development of each is the condition for the free development of all."** None will be left behind or enslaved or oppressed. The revolution will radically change both human nature and history.

SOCRATES: So human nature is changeable.

MARX: Yes.

SOCRATES: Why, then, can it never change *before* the revolution? Why couldn't a selfish man become an unselfish man before 1848? Haven't sinners ever become saints? And why not more than one man? And why not a whole society of such unselfish and peaceful men?

MARX: Because the sufficient cause of such a change awaits the revolution. Moral and religious appeals have not accomplished it. They remain abstract ideals, not concrete realities, until the social structure is radically altered. Selfish social structures make selfish individuals.

SOCRATES: I wonder whether it makes sense to use the word "selfish" to describe, not just a man, but a social structure.

MARX: Yet it does make sense. A selfish social structure is one that necessitates class conflict. An unselfish social structure is one free of class conflict.

SOCRATES: Why can't we act unselfishly even if we live in a "selfish social structure"?

MARX: Because we are all determined to act as we do by our social structures.

SOCRATES: That is the claim we must now investigate.

5

Do Saints Refute Communism?

SOCRATES: Have you ever heard of saints?

MARX: You may as well speak to me of spooks, Socrates.

SOCRATES: But saints are empirical data, unlike spooks. Data that seem to refute your theory. For some very good men have lived in some very bad societies. One of them, Thomas More, once wrote, "The times are never so bad but that a good man can live in them."

MARX: That is his opinion. Idealistic words prove nothing. My philosophy is based on science, not religion; on hard fact, not sweet dreams.

SOCRATES: We have had occasion to question that claim once already. I think we had better test it again. Tell me, Karl, what about you? Did you live in bad times?

MARX: Indeed I did.

SOCRATES: And did you try the experiment of attempting to live as a saint in these times?

MARX: Why do you ask such a silly question, Socrates?

SOCRATES: Because that would have given you at least some experimental data to test your theory that such a thing is impossible.

MARX: What do you think I am, a *Catholic?*

SOCRATES: I thought you had been a Protestant for a while, when you were young.

MARX: I tried to be—when I was young and foolish.

SOCRATES: But you were born a Jew, without trying to be one, weren't you?

MARX: My father repudiated his Judaism.

SOCRATES: I know your history. The point is simply that you made no experiment and did not bother to investigate the many experiments made by others, experiments in sanctity, experiments that did produce data relevant to your theory, data that seem to contradict it. But Thomas More did exactly that.

MARX: So you blame me now for not sharing his idealistic beliefs?

SOCRATES: No, I only label his opinion as more scientific, because it is based on historical data. And I label yours as religious, because it is not.

MARX: That is outrageous and grossly unjust!

SOCRATES: I agree.

MARX: What?

SOCRATES: I agree that for you to appropriate the label "scientific" from the place where it belongs —Thomas More's idea—and to claim it for your untested idea is indeed outrageous and grossly unjust. It is theft.

MARX: No, you are the thief who steals and misplaces labels. Even if my ideas are not scientific—which they are—they certainly are not *religious*! (Spit! Sput! Sputter!)

SOCRATES: Well, then, let us test *that* claim of yours.

MARX: You never give up, do you?

SOCRATES: No. Tell me, how would you define a "religious" belief?

MARX: As an idiotic, alienating, dehumanizing myth to drug passive and weak minds.

SOCRATES: Perhaps we should first define "definition" so that we can distinguish it from "denunciation" or "defamation".

MARX: What's *your* definition, then?

SOCRATES: There is nothing "mine" or "yours" about a definition. It is not private property but common.

MARX: There is nothing in common between bourgeois definitions of such key ideas and Communist definitions.

SOCRATES: So according to Communism, there is nothing in common? How ironic that *you*, the Communist, would make into private property that which others would hold in common—in the world of ideas, at least.

MARX: We Communists are concerned with real property, Socrates; you philosophers are concerned with ideas.

SOCRATES: We must discuss the status of ideas some time later: whether they are real or unreal. But for now, we must finish our business at hand: Will you accept the dictionary's definition of a religious belief as a definition that is at least verbally held in common, or agreed to?

MARX: Let's say I do, just for practical purposes.

SOCRATES: Well, then, the dictionary tells us that the word "religion" means literally "relating" or "relation" or "binding" or "binding back".

MARX: Frankly, Socrates, I am not interested in either religion or etymology. So what?

SOCRATES: So this is what a religious belief is according to the dictionary, which reports how words are in fact popularly used. A religious belief is a belief about a relationship with a religious object, with God or something Godlike, whether that object is real or unreal. Is that an acceptable definition to you?

MARX: Yes, but it is also essential to religion to be unscientific. I want to include that in the definition, too.

SOCRATES: All right. How about this, then? Religious beliefs will not allow themselves to be refuted by any empirical data because these beliefs are not based on empirical data.

MARX: Good. I agree completely.

SOCRATES: Well, then, let us apply our agreed definition of religion to the question we were discussing, about Thomas More's belief that sanctity is possible even in wicked societies. It is clearly a religious question because it is about a man's relationship with God. And More based his belief, that sanctity was possible even in the worst of times, on the data of his own life and the lives of the saints he studied. But you base your opposing belief about the same thing on no data at all, and you will not allow this data, the data of this saint or other saints, to refute your belief. So I conclude that your belief that all men are determined by their social structures is a religious belief.

6

The Question of Freedom

MARX: I care not how you label my belief. It is true.

SOCRATES: Not if it contains a contradiction.

MARX: What contradiction?

SOCRATES: You yourself, I think.

MARX: I don't understand.

SOCRATES: I think that your idea cannot account for its own origin.

MARX: What origin?

SOCRATES: You. You wrote this *Manifesto*, did you not?

MARX: Yes.

SOCRATES: And you said that you were the first to discover the fundamental formula for human history: past oppression and present opportunity and the future triumph of Communism, didn't you?

MARX: Yes.

SOCRATES: And one of these ideas, one of the principles of your philosophy, is that all ideas are determined by social conditions, especially class structures, isn't that right?

MARX: Correct.

SOCRATES: And not the other way round, as the idealists think?

MARX: Correct again.

SOCRATES: Now you were born into a bourgeois society and a bourgeois family, a typical "middle class" family, weren't you? And Engels, too?

MARX: Yes.

SOCRATES: Can you tell me the name of a single Communist thinker or political activist whom you knew of in your lifetime whose origin was not bourgeois but proletarian?

MARX: Oh, in their youth they were bourgeois. But they rejected their bourgeois origins; they saw the light. As even you could do, Socrates. You would be a great asset to our movement.

SOCRATES: You seem to appeal to my free choice.

MARX: You will not trick me there. Free will is an illusion. Science knows only determinism. Whatever we do and whatever we choose and whatever we think, we are both only instruments of history.

SOCRATES: But here is something I do not understand: you, and every Communist of your day, came from the bourgeoisie. And you say that individuals cannot help acting and thinking and choosing as they do, because it is their social class that determines everything. If we accept both those premises, we arrive at the conclusion that Communist ideas and actions are thoroughly bourgeois!

MARX: That conclusion is so disgusting that I can think of only one word to describe it: it is bourgeois!

SOCRATES: But I own no means of producing any wealth. So by definition I cannot be a member of this hated class. In fact, I was poor all my life.

MARX: So?

SOCRATES: But you just called my idea that *your* Communist ideas must be bourgeois a bourgeois idea.

MARX: So?

SOCRATES: And you say that all ideas are determined by class.

MARX: They are.

SOCRATES: So how can my "bourgeois" ideas come from my proletarian class background? And how can your proletarian ideas come from your bourgeois class background?

MARX: I have repudiated my background, and you have repudiated yours.

SOCRATES: Did your bourgeois society and teachers and parents tell you to repudiate them?

MARX: Of course not.

SOCRATES: They wanted you to conform, to be as bourgeois as they were.

MARX: Yes.

SOCRATES: But you wanted to rebel.

MARX: Yes.

SOCRATES: So it seems that individuals do have the power of free choice after all! You yourself are an example of it.

MARX: No, that does not follow. I chose, yes. But that choice was just as necessary, just as much determined by the fate of the historical dialectic, as the choices of the others to remain bourgeois. Fate chose me and not them as the instrument to propagate Communism.

SOCRATES: So there is no freedom for anyone at all, according to your philosophy?

MARX: That is not so. But in order to understand how this is not so, we must do the thing you always insist on doing: we must define our terms. We use the same word, but not the same meaning. When you say "freedom", you are thinking of *bourgeois* freedom, not Communist freedom.

SOCRATES: Then what is Communist freedom?

MARX: Under Communism, and only under Communism, everyone will be free: free from want and war, free from crime and joblessness and homelessness and poverty.

SOCRATES: Will they be free to think non-Communist thoughts?

MARX: That is not true freedom. Wait, Socrates. Before you reply to that, let me explain. You don't understand the Communist notion of freedom because you begin with your assumption of one universal, unchangeable human nature or essence; and you then ask whether this possesses freedom. But there is no such thing as an unchanging human nature, or "species-being", as I call it.

SOCRATES: So you believe there are no real species; that universal words like "man" or "river" as distinct from individual words like "Socrates" or "Nile" do not refer to any common realities or universal natures. You are a nominalist. You believe that universality is found only in words, in *nomina*.

MARX: That is correct. So there is no one "freedom" or "justice" common to all classes and stages of humanity. As history moves along its dialectical way, and as society changes its class structures, different forms of humanity, and therefore of freedom and of justice, are produced, depending on the different forms of property.

SOCRATES: But whether humanity comes in one form or in many forms, you must speak of forms and, thus, of universality. Even if bourgeois humanity and Communist humanity are two species rather than one, there are still species. And one Communist falls under the same species as another Communist.

MARX: How I solve the abstract logical problem of universal terms is not important. What is important is that each stage of history produces a different kind of freedom. That's what we are talking about now, after all.

SOCRATES: So under Capitalism there is no freedom from poverty, crime, or war, as there is under Communism.

MARX: Correct.

SOCRATES: And the reason for that is because Capitalism is still based on class conflict.

MARX: Yes. You do understand.

SOCRATES: And under Communism there is no free market economy, or free trade, as there is under Capitalism—and for the same reason: no classes.

MARX: Correct again.

SOCRATES: Well, let us accept your definitions and proceed to evaluate them. I do not claim to know much about what you call the Capitalist form of freedom, and therefore I cannot judge whether it is good or bad, although at first appearance it seems to be a good thing. But I do know that the freedom that you claim is given by Communism—freedom from poverty and crime and war—is a good. For it is naturally desired by all sane men.

MARX: You are coming to agree with me more and more.

SOCRATES: But I still do not know whether or not you are right in claiming that Communism really gives men these freedoms and that Capitalism does not.

But I am most interested in neither of these two kinds of freedom but rather in a third kind, which I would call freedom of thought. So I ask you whether there is freedom of thought under Communism.

MARX: There is not.

SOCRATES: You freely admit this?

MARX: Yes. But I also say that it does not exist under Capitalism, either. It is a ghost, a myth, like thought itself. It is an effect, not a cause. The thought of any society is a by-product of its economic class structure. It does not fly free, like an angel, with no roots in its social soil.

SOCRATES: This is a crucial question, and we must return to it later, at the point where it comes up in your book. We have digressed from that book for a long time now, and we should find our way back. But before we do, I must ask you this one question: I still do not understand how your Communist thoughts grew necessarily from your bourgeois social soil.

MARX: I will try to explain it to you more clearly. I am not the cause of the Revolution, nor is my book, nor are my thoughts. Those are only instruments. They are the matches that ignite the fire that will spread through the world. It will spread of necessity, by its own nature, because the world's dead leaves— the dying products of Capitalism—are lying withered and dead on the ground. It is their destiny to be burned, because it is the very nature of Capitalism to be self-destructive and the very nature of Communism to triumph. For Capitalism produces its own gravediggers in the proletariat.

SOCRATES: I understand how a thing can destroy itself, I think, whether that thing is a single person or a social system. But I do not understand how a thing can create itself. Do you?

MARX: Of course not. Nothing can create itself or cause itself. That is a scientific impossibility.

SOCRATES: I agree. So what is the origin of Communism, then? You say that only one little match is needed—your *Manifesto*—and the effect will be the destruction of the whole Capitalist world, by the fire of revolution. But who drops the first match? Does it drop itself? Does it create itself? Does your book write itself?

MARX: Of course not.

SOCRATES: You write the book. You drop the match. So you are the cause of the fire.

MARX: Of course I am. But I am only an instrument, a link in history's causal chain. I do not believe in the "great man theory of history". There is among men no Prometheus, no Hercules, no Zeus who moves worlds. We are moved by our world. We are our destiny.

SOCRATES: And your destiny is to be the prophet of Communism.

MARX: If you insist on using religious language, yes.

SOCRATES: That is, the prophet of the philosophy that teaches that all men are determined in their actions, and even their thoughts, by their class system, their social system, their economic system.

MARX: Yes.

SOCRATES: So there *is* no such thing as free thought. Thought is just as much an effect of social conditions as wealth is.

MARX: Exactly.

SOCRATES: So a man does not have free will to choose which thoughts he will think or which acts he will perform.

MARX: He has will and choice, but they are not free. They are not independent of the causal chains that bind him. And those chains are social.

SOCRATES: I see. So everything, in your system, is accounted for, is explained, by necessary causes.

MARX: Yes. That is why my system is scientific. I leave nothing uncaused, nothing unaccounted for, nothing unexplained.

SOCRATES: I think there is one thing you have left unexplained.

MARX: What?

SOCRATES: Yourself, as the writer of this book and the thinker of these thoughts.

MARX: I told you already, Socrates: I was only an instrument. Thoughts as well as acts, and human acts as well as the acts of animals and plants and minerals, are all necessary, not free. Everything is predetermined by the causal chains.

SOCRATES: Necessarily, rather than freely?

MARX: Yes.

SOCRATES: And if these chains bind necessarily rather than freely, then it is impossible for them not to work, not to bind, not to produce their effects?

MARX: Yes.

SOCRATES: Including every detail, even by what means the effects come about and when?

MARX: Even that. There can be no exception, no tiny crack through which there can seep some transcendental, incommensurable anfractuosity—

SOCRATES: Speak simply, please!

MARX: For instance, we cannot say that the revolution is inevitable rather than free but at the same time say that *when* it happens, or *how* it happens, is free. That would be unscientific. It is only some of the future that we can presently know and predict, so we can know that the revolution will happen but not when. But that which we do not know will also actually happen. And whatever happens will happen by causal necessity, not outside it.

SOCRATES: So you will not allow the slightest little nook or cranny in your system for free choice?

MARX: Not one.

SOCRATES: Not even for one tiny event?

MARX: No.

SOCRATES: Like the dropping of a match?

MARX: No.

SOCRATES: Then why drop it?

MARX: What do you mean?

SOCRATES: If the fire of revolution and its time and its every detail are all necessary and unchangeable; if there is nothing you can do to hinder the revolution or to add to its inevitability; if all is predestined, why not just eat, drink, and be merry, instead of devoting your life to Communism? Why make sacrifices for Communism if nothing can stop it anyway? Why pay for something if you can get it for free?

MARX: Socrates, I was wrong.

SOCRATES: About freedom?

MARX: No, about you. I thought you were beginning to understand me.

SOCRATES: Alas, I think you are right there. You are right about where you were wrong. I *don't* understand you. Is that my fate?

MARX: For now, yes. But perhaps your fate is to see the light and join me soon. And if you do, you will understand.

SOCRATES: But not until then?

MARX: Probably not.

SOCRATES: So you say that understanding itself means a different thing to Communists from what it means to non-Communists?

MARX: Yes, indeed.

SOCRATES: So I would have to become a Communist in order to understand it, rather than understanding it first in order then to decide whether to become a Communist?

MARX: Exactly.

SOCRATES: What you say is strangely similar to what the religious mystics say. They say that you must first become a mystic, and only then can you understand mysticism. And some say the same about religious faith: that "unless you believe, you will not understand."

MARX: But religion is idealism, not materialistic science. Religion gets everything backward. It does not know that thought and understanding are effects rather than causes. Communism *as a reality* is not the effect of Communism *as a thought*, but vice versa.

SOCRATES: So the Communist revolution, and all other revolutions, too, do not begin in thought?

MARX: No. They begin in the streets.

SOCRATES: But why do men take to the streets to revolt unless they are moved to do so by a thought that this revolution is good or wise or desirable? These are the thoughts they do have, in fact, are they not?

MARX: Oh, yes, they do have such thoughts. But the thoughts cannot arise unless they are in turn caused by real material conditions. And when the thoughts do arise, they cannot cause material events. How could a thought spill blood? How could a thing like a ghost push the buttons of a machine like the human body?

SOCRATES: That is indeed a great mystery: how our thoughts cause physical events in our own bodies.

MARX: It is worse than a mystery: it is an utter irrationality. It is an impossibility.

SOCRATES: But if you are scientific; you begin with the data, not with a theory, isn't that true?

MARX: Yes.

SOCRATES: But you seem to deny the data that we all experience: the power of thought to cause and motivate us to act. You deny this mysterious and difficult data in order to preserve your rational-seeming theory of determinism and materialism. So, once again I conclude that your thought is not scientific but more like a religious faith.

MARX: Socrates, this is outrageous.

SOCRATES: You have said it.

7

What Has Capitalism Wrought?

SOCRATES: For too long we have been sailing far away from the land of your book in the boat of our conversation. We should return to the dock to take aboard more provisions from the book.

MARX: It's about time. And it's also about time to think about time, about history, about real events instead of those abstract logical arguments of yours. After all, we're supposed to be discussing my book and my ideology, not yours.

SOCRATES: The matter is yours; the logical form is neither mine nor yours but universal and inescapable. All right, we shall do what you suggest. For the next step in the argument of the *Manifesto* is your summary of what you say the bourgeoisie has already done. And this is very concrete. You say: **"The bourgeoisie, wherever it has got the upper hand, has put an end to all feudal, patriarchal, idyllic relations. It has pitilessly torn asunder the motley feudal ties that bound man to his 'natural superiors', and has left remaining no other nexus between man and man than naked self-interest, than callous 'cash payment'."** Let's make that point no. 1, about social relationships.

"It has drowned the most heavenly ecstasies of religious fervour, of chivalrous enthusiasm, of

philistine sentimentalism, in the icy water of egotistical calculation." Let's make that point no. 2,
about religious feelings.

"It has resolved personal worth into exchange
value." Let's make that point no. 3, about personal
worth.

"And in place of the numberless indefeasible
chartered freedoms, [it] has set up that single, un-
conscionable freedom—Free Trade." Let's make
that point no. 4, about freedom.

"In one word, for exploitation, veiled by religious and political illusions, it has substituted
naked, direct, brutal exploitation." I think that is
not a new specific point, just your general summary
of all the points.

"The bourgeoisie has stripped of its halo every
occupation hitherto honoured and looked up to
with reverent awe. It has converted the physician,
the lawyer, the priest, the poet, the man of science, into its paid wage-labourers." Let's make
that point no. 5, about occupations.

"The bourgeoisie has torn away from the family its sentimental veil, and has reduced the family relation to a mere money relation." Let's make
that point no. 6, about the family.

Then, a bit later, you say: "The bourgeoisie has
subjected the country to the rule of the towns.
It has created enormous cities, has greatly in-
creased the urban population as compared with
the rural, and has thus rescued a considerable
part of the population from the idiocy of rural
life." Let's make that point no. 7, about town and
country.

"Just as it has made the country dependent on the towns, so it has made barbarian and semi-barbarian countries dependent on the civilized ones, nations of peasants on nations of bourgeoisie, the East on the West." Let's make that point no. 8, about globalization.

MARX: Surely you see why I call these changes **"revolutionary"**. They are all changes that I observed in my world, changes that had already proved revolutionary, changes that ended the medieval society and produced the modern one.

SOCRATES: Indeed. But I have three questions about your description of them.

First, did all these things in fact happen?

Second, if they did, was their cause the bourgeoisie, as you say it was?

Third, do you say these changes were good or bad? For the better or for the worse? Do you praise them or condemn them? You seem to do both.

MARX: The first question is easy to answer, Socrates, unless you are blind. It's a fact, not an opinion.

SOCRATES: I hope you will excuse me for not simply accepting that on your authority. It's a settled habit of mine, you see: as another philosopher wrote, "Test all things, hold fast to that which is good." Or, in my own words, "The unexamined life is not worth living."

MARX: Do what you must, then.

SOCRATES: I will. Let's review what you say the bourgeoisie has done.

First, it **"has left remaining no other nexus between man and man than naked self-interest, than callous 'cash payment'."** So you are claiming that bourgeois Romeos say to bourgeois Juliets, not "I love you", but "How much do you cost?"

Second, **"it has drowned the most heavenly ecstasies of religious fervour."** So you claim there are no saints or mystics left in bourgeois societies.

Third, **"it has resolved personal worth into exchange value."** So you claim that nurses, social workers, and the like no longer serve the poor and weak because they see them as having any personal worth but only because of their **"exchange value"**. They think they will get rich from the poor somehow.

Fourth, it has converted all freedoms into free trade. So you claim that Capitalism has abolished all previous freedoms as no previous tyrant was able to do and has created a new one, as no previous merchants were able to do.

Fifth, **"it has converted the physician, the lawyer, the priest, the poet, the man of science, into its paid wage-labourers."** So you claim that Capitalism has removed the love of health from physicians, the love of justice from lawyers, the love of God from priests, the love of beauty from poets, and the love of truth from scientists. None of these love his work any more, only his wage. And you say that this radical change of attitude happened just because the economy is now based on interest or capital.

Sixth, it **"has reduced the family relation to a mere money relation."** So you claim that the new economy has erased one of nature's strongest instincts, the love and loyalty between spouses and siblings and even mother-love. I see why you call this radical and revolutionary: a change in human nature itself, even in human instincts.

MARX: I'm glad you see my point, Socrates.

SOCRATES: And you claim to have observed all this as a fact in your own day.

MARX: Yes.

SOCRATES: Even though almost no one else did.

MARX: I saw the seed. Others saw the grown plant.

SOCRATES: So the next century or two would make this seed grow to a size where everyone could see it.

MARX: Yes.

SOCRATES: And that makes it a scientific claim, an empirically testable claim.

MARX: Yes.

SOCRATES: So that if this did not happen—if, let's say, 150 years after you wrote, few or none of these changes had clearly taken place, this would falsify your claim.

MARX: Yes.

SOCRATES: You may be in for some shocking surprises when you learn more history. But that is not my purpose now. Let us proceed to my second question. You say the cause of this revolution is a new socio-economic system, Capitalism.

MARX: Yes. And I know what you will say next, Socrates. You will ask how such a tiny cause could produce such an enormous effect. You will ask whether the effect exceeds the power of the cause, thus violating a basic principle of science.

SOCRATES: You are right. That is exactly what I was going to say.

MARX: Well, I was the first to discover this surprising fact.

SOCRATES: That this cause *is* strong enough to produce this effect? Or that that basic principle of science is not true?

MARX: That this cause is strong enough. In fact, it is strong enough to account for everything in human history. Economic determinism is what makes history a science.

SOCRATES: So economics is a "first cause".

MARX: Yes.

SOCRATES: Like God.

MARX: No, not like God. Darwin and I, between us, eliminated God: he from nature, I from history. I sent Darwin a copy of my book, you know.

SOCRATES: I know. I also know that he never replied.

MARX: You know quite a bit.

SOCRATES: I also know *why* he never replied.

MARX: How do you know that?

SOCRATES: I have conversed with him.

MARX: Oh.

SOCRATES: Would you like to know what he thought of your book?

MARX: It is of no consequence.

SOCRATES: What do you think of *his* book? Do you accept his theory of evolution?

MARX: Yes, I do.

SOCRATES: So you say that once there was no life, and then, many centuries later, there was. And once there was only subhuman life, and then, many centuries later, there was human life.

MARX: Yes. It evolved by natural selection. You can even see analogies between natural selection and the historical dialectic—

SOCRATES: I see that. But I also see something else, I think. Please consider these three things that you say you believe. First, you believe in evolution. Second, you do not believe in a God, a Creator or First Cause or Designing Mind behind evolution. Third, you believe in the scientific principle of causality: that effects cannot exceed their causes, that nothing comes to be without an adequate cause—in fact, you would say even a necessary and deterministic cause. Do you believe these three things?

MARX: Yes.

SOCRATES: Do you see a problem here?

MARX: I am a step ahead of you, Socrates. You are going to say that there is a logical contradiction in accepting all three of these ideas. For if effects cannot exceed their causes, then the living cannot be caused by the nonliving, and higher life forms cannot be caused merely by lower, nor intelligence by something without intelligence, nor plan and design and order by blind chance, unless these lesser causes are only instruments of a greater, divine cause. And so I must either give up evolution, or give up atheism and admit a God to explain it.

SOCRATES: What a remarkably clear way of putting the problem! Do you have an equally clear solution?

MARX: I do. A God would totally undermine my whole scientific materialism, so atheism is non-negotiable. And the same reason justifies my belief in evolution: it is the only alternative to divine design in explaining the order in nature. It is science's trump card in its ongoing battle against religion and superstition. So if there is indeed a logical tension among these three ideas, we must modify the most abstract and general principle of the three, the principle of causality, or else modify an even more abstract and general principle that we must assume if there is to be any problem at all in accepting all three of these ideas: namely, the logical law of non-contradiction. Perhaps logical contradictions are the way history moves. Perhaps we must learn to accept logical tensions rather than avoid them.

SOCRATES: How interesting! In the name of science you would modify one or both of the two most fundamental principles of science, either the principle of causality or the law of logical non-contradiction. Can you name me one successful and recognized scientist in all of history who has ever made that move?

MARX: I think I am the first.

SOCRATES: But there are many scientists who deny your atheism.

MARX: Yes . . .

SOCRATES: And there are some scientists who deny natural selection.

MARX: Perhaps. And both are very foolish.

SOCRATES: Perhaps. But they are *scientists*. Would not most of them say that you deny two of science's most unquestionable principles for the sake of two of science's most questionable theories?

MARX: No, they would not say that unless they were fools. I care not what they say. I have seen something in history that they have not seen.

SOCRATES: Let us return to that claim, then. You claim to have seen a catastrophic change in human nature itself wrought by the bourgeoisie. This is a change so radical that the only other theory in the history of human thought that has ever proposed a more radical historical change in human nature is a theory in Christian theology: I mean the idea of Adam's Fall. The more I examine your philosophy, the more parallels I seem to see in it to religion.

MARX: Is your purpose insult or argument?

SOCRATES: Argument, I assure you. And my question now is very simple about this radical revolution that you describe. You ascribe its cause to the bourgeoisie. (What a compliment you give to your enemy, by the way! What a tremendous power you ascribe to it!)

MARX: What's your question, Socrates? You're meandering again.

SOCRATES: Simply this: Is it true? Is it a fact that needs a cause to explain it at all? Has it really happened?

MARX: It all really did happen, Socrates, I assure you. Shall we look at the eight points again?

SOCRATES: No, we should look at how we should look at them. At least the first six of them. I listed eight points, but I did not question the last two because we know they happened by empirical observation: the concentrating of population in towns and cities and the concentrating of power in the most modern, that is technologically advanced, nations. Those two changes are external and easily observable. The other six are internal and more radical changes, changes in human nature itself. I wonder how you can prove them, since they are not directly observable. Where are your data?

MARX: They *are* observable. I rely on no other method of proof, only scientific observation and prediction. Of course, a short pamphlet like the *Manifesto* has no room for the mass of data I gathered in *Capital*.

SOCRATES: I was not asking what *book* to look in for your data, but where you found it in the world.

MARX: Everywhere.

SOCRATES: Well, let's look. Which were the most advanced, the most bourgeois nations in your day?

MARX: Germany and England, and perhaps the northeast of America.

SOCRATES: And your data is empirical observation.

MARX: It is.

SOCRATES: Is your data present, or is it also future?

MARX: What do you mean?

SOCRATES: Do you claim to observe the future directly, like a prophet, or only to predict it on the basis of your observations of the present?

MARX: The present, of course.

SOCRATES: Then let us look at the countries you named in the era that was your present. Do we find there the features you say were already produced by bourgeois Capitalism? Do we find no personal friendships or loyalties, no religion, slavery rather than its abolition, no love of career or vocation, and no family relationships except monetary ones? For instance, in the novels that depict life in England or Germany or America in your century, do any of them share your picture of human life under the bourgeoisie?

MARX: They do not see as deeply as I do. They look at the leaves that are still on the tree; I see that they are withered and destined to fall off. They see the tree, I see its inner rot, the dying from within. I am a better doctor than they, if they do not see that the patient—bourgeois society—is terminally ill.

SOCRATES: And your prognosis is based on science, not on anything like religion?

MARX: Yes. The scientific evidence is summarized in *Capital*.

SOCRATES: Fortunately for both of us, our task is not to examine that book here, in either its details or its arguments, but only its conclusion. Would you accept this as a fair summary of its practical historical conclusion, your prognosis for bourgeois Capitalism? Something like this: that bourgeois Capitalism was already dying in your time and that it was doomed to expire forever at some time in the near future?

MARX: Yes. I may have exaggerated and oversimplified a bit in the *Manifesto*—after all, it was short, popular, rhetorical, and designed to rouse the masses, not to provide scientific detail for the scholar.

SOCRATES: But you stand by all its essential points?

MARX: Of course.

SOCRATES: I think it is time for you to learn a bit of history.

8

What Has
Communism Wrought?

SOCRATES: What would you say, then, if I told you that in the next 150 years after your death bourgeois Capitalism would grow continually in both size and power, especially in the most advanced nations, with only a few interruptions and crises, until at the turn of the millennium it would be the only economically successful system on earth, with no signs of decay or revolution or even dissatisfaction, and every sign of unending stability?

MARX: Is this true, or are you testing me with a thought experiment?

SOCRATES: It is true, I assure you.

MARX: If it is, then I say I am extremely surprised at how long the patient took to die and at how long we Communists must patiently wait for the inevitable.

SOCRATES: And what would you say if I told you that Communism would succeed with its revolution, not in the advanced nations of Europe or America, but in the poor nations, especially China and Russia?

MARX: The location would be another surprise, but not the success. Tell me more about the success.

SOCRATES: Communism ruled nearly half the world for the better part of the twentieth century.

MARX: Now that is a more believable and predictable scenario! So Capitalism eventually died?

SOCRATES: No. Communism did, after ruling half the world.

MARX: Impossible! How? By another revolution?

SOCRATES: Not one drop of blood was shed.

MARX: How then could it die?

SOCRATES: No one believed it any more.

MARX: You lie! You are toying with me!

SOCRATES: You know this is not so. We *cannot* lie in this place.

MARX: Why did they cease to believe? Did religion replace science, and superstition replace reason, and monkish contemplation replace practicality?

SOCRATES: No, just the opposite. Men ceased to believe in it because it did not work.

MARX: What do you mean?

SOCRATES: It did not free the proletariat but enslaved them, both economically and politically. It was put in place only by force and was kept in place only by force. Whole peoples were massacred. One man alone killed fifty million political enemies. Another killed one-third of his country's people. Never in human history was there a more enormous slaughter of human life and human happiness. Never in human history was any system hated and feared by more people.

MARX: How could this happen?

SOCRATES: Because your politics stemmed from the French Revolution, and once your disciples achieved power, they instituted reigns of terror just as the Jacobins had, but on a far larger scale. No other system in modern history was more unstable than your system of international socialism, except one, a system called national socialism.

MARX: What happened to bourgeois Capitalism?

SOCRATES: No economic system in human history was ever accepted and used with more satisfaction and success by more people.

MARX: Now I know I am in a dream: a nightmare. These things *cannot* be true. Yet in this world they *are*. I know you cannot lie here, as you say—though how I know this, I know not. I cannot endure this world, whatever it is, dream or not. How can I escape? I would rather be dead in my own world than alive in this one.

SOCRATES: You cannot escape. You have already died. *This* is your world now, the world of truth, not of lies or dreams.

MARX: Where are the factories? Where are the wages? Where are the politics?

SOCRATES: As I said, this is the world of truth, not of lies or dreams. You must learn to live in it.

MARX: If this is all true, then history has refuted me as thoroughly as I can possibly imagine anyone ever being refuted—refuted not just by principles and arguments but by concrete consequences.

SOCRATES: Yes. Ideas have consequences.

MARX: I taught that ideas *were* consequences.

SOCRATES: You know now some of the terrible consequences of that teaching.

MARX: But how can we go on? How can I still argue with you and defend the rest of my book?

SOCRATES: You must confront and understand all that you have thought and written and done. You believed in fate and not free choice. Well, this is your fate, and you have no free choice about it. You cannot escape yourself here, as you could on earth.

MARX: What must be must be, then. So what must we do next?

SOCRATES: Why, finish what we started, of course. We were investigating three questions about the revolution you said the bourgeoisie had wrought.

The first question was whether the catastrophic things you said happened did in fact already happen in your time; and, if not, whether they would soon happen and become clearly visible later. We have already seen the answer to this question; it has been settled, not by argument, but by history. It is your own chosen god, history, who judges you.

The second question was whether the bourgeoisie could be powerful enough to cause all these effects, or whether, instead, other forces might not have more power to bring happiness or unhappiness to human individuals and families, relationships, and communities. That is a very large question, and we should discuss it at length sometime, especially because the vast majority disagree with you there. Is the economic system really so Godlike, so omnipotent and omnipresent?

But we have already taken too many detours, and we must focus on your book, so I will confine myself to my third question now. You say the bourgeoisie have abolished things you describe as **"idyllic"** and **"reverent"** and replaced them with things you describe as **"pitiless"**, **"naked self-interest"**, **"callous"**, **"icy"**, **"egotistical"**, **"shameless"**, and **"brutal"**.

MARX: So what is your question about what I say there?

SOCRATES: Are you *glad* that this **"brutal"** thing has destroyed this **"idyllic"** thing?

MARX: Yes.

SOCRATES: Because it is good or because it is evil? Is this brutal thing your hero or your villain? If it is your hero, why do you admire the **"brutal"** more than the **"idyllic"**? If it is your villain, why do you say you are glad it has triumphed?

MARX: You don't understand, Socrates: good and evil are relative to history, not static, timeless abstract ideas. From the feudal point of view, bourgeois Capitalism was evil, because it destroyed feudalism. But from the Communist point of view, it was good because it paved the way for Communism.

SOCRATES: So things that all men would consider evil—even horribly evil—like torture and massive massacres and deliberate lies—these become good simply by being useful for your revolution?

MARX: As I said, Socrates, good and evil are historically relative.

SOCRATES: Does that mean that your answer to my question is "Yes"?

MARX: Yes.

SOCRATES: So anything—anything at all—changes from evil to good when it is a means to the Communist end?

MARX: There must be *some* absolute, Socrates, some end to justify all the means. For some it is God or family or the social status quo. For some it is their own private happiness. A man must serve some cause, some end.

SOCRATES: True. But do you not distinguish between ends that liberate and ends that enslave?

MARX: Indeed I do! All past history is enslavement; only Communism is liberation.

SOCRATES: Even if by ordinary standards, even if by all other, non-Communist standards, it is exactly the opposite? Even if all human beings except Communists hate it?

MARX: Truth is relative, Socrates.

SOCRATES: Is that true?

MARX: It is.

SOCRATES: Absolutely?

9

Is Communism Predestination?

SOCRATES: It will be pointless to explore the details of your prophecies about what would happen to the bourgeoisie and the proletariat and to the class structures of society and to its economy, since these predictions are no longer matters of argument but matters of historical fact here. But we must examine your *philosophy* of history.

MARX: I must interrupt, Socrates. I do not understand. What year are we in right now?

SOCRATES: We do not measure time that way here.

MARX: Then how do you know history?

SOCRATES: All historical times on earth are past times to us here.

MARX: So you know everything? Like God?

SOCRATES: No. Each individual knows only as much as he needs to know of that vast sum of all times that I have called past times here.

MARX: I do not understand how that can be.

SOCRATES: You do not need to. You only need to understand yourself and your thoughts. So let us summarize your essential argument about why the revolution is inevitable. You wrote:

All previous historical movements were movements of minorities, or in the interest of minorities. The proletarian movement is the self-conscious, independent movement of the immense majority, in the interest of the immense majority.

Do you really mean this? Do you believe this is true?

MARX: Of course I do. Are you suggesting that I am a liar and a hypocrite?

SOCRATES: Certainly not.

MARX: You trust me, then?

SOCRATES: Only two minds know with certainty whether you lie: One of them you do not know. And you simpy could not bring yourself to believe in his existence even now. But that is not necessary; for the other one you do know. That is you yourself. My purpose is only to help you to "know thyself" better, by judging not you but your book.

MARX: Then what is your question about my book?

SOCRATES: If you believe what you have written here, then it would be in Communism's own interests to support democracy everywhere, with free elections and referenda.

MARX: We do support free elections.

SOCRATES: Then why do you rely on the political power of a small minority, a power elite, and ultimately on the physical power of what you call **"the violent overthrow of the bourgeoisie"**?

MARX: As a means to the end, of course. It is the proletarians' will that we Communists serve. We serve the people; they do not serve us.

SOCRATES: Is "the proletarians' will" the will of the majority?

MARX: Yes.

SOCRATES: But the majority don't like you! They don't like Communism.

MARX: Deep down they do. For everyone is in favor of his own best interests, and we serve those interests.

SOCRATES: But *they* do not think you do. So you must impose your will by force, whether you are right or wrong about Communism serving their best interests.

MARX: The psychological point is moot, Socrates. We need not argue about souls and minds and wills. The proletarians themselves will take our argument out of our mouths and into the streets. They themselves will rise up and overthrow their oppressors.

SOCRATES: Even if they do not feel oppressed?

MARX: Of course they feel oppressed.

SOCRATES: You have reasons for this belief of yours, I suppose?

MARX: Of course.

SOCRATES: I'll bet you can guess what my next question is going to be.

MARX: I'll tell you the reasons—my reasons and theirs, for they are identical. For one thing—as I wrote in that same section—**"The proletarian is without property."**

SOCRATES: None at all, of any kind?

MARX: Only a slight exaggeration. Also, **"his relation to his wife and children has no longer anything in common with the bourgeois family relations."**

SOCRATES: Nothing at all?

MARX: Socrates, the *Manifesto* is a popular pamphlet. Slight exaggerations and oversimplifications are necessary.

SOCRATES: Go on reading, please.

MARX: **"Modern industrial labour, modern subjection to capital . . . has stripped him of every trace of national character."**

SOCRATES: So you say the poor are less patriotic than the rich? Shall we investigate this claim with statistics?

MARX: It's a pamphlet, Socrates, not a scholarly statistics sheet. It's also about where the world is going, not about where it already is. It's the direction of the future.

SOCRATES: So you predict an end to nationalism.

MARX: Not only to nationalism, but to nations.

SOCRATES: And, therefore, to wars.

MARX: Yes. The last war will be the worldwide revolution of the proletariat in all countries, against not only the bourgeoisie but also against bourgeois nationality itself.

SOCRATES: Go on with your description of proletarian life in bourgeois nations. We must see your full picture if we are to compare it fairly with the facts.

MARX: Also, **"law, morality, religion, are to him so many bourgeois prejudices."** You will note, Socrates, that I have been as specific as a short pamphlet allows in defining **"oppression"**. And that I have logically arranged these specifics in a hierarchy, from the most to the least important.

SOCRATES: But to most of the proletariat themselves the last point is the most important, not the least.

MARX: My analysis is not psychological but historical. I rank them by causal power. Property relations cause these intermediate features such as nations and law. Morality and religion are the weakest effects down at the bottom of the chain.

SOCRATES: We will be sure to return to this central philosophical claim of yours later. But for now I want to ask you only one purely factual question.

MARX: Ask away, Socrates. Facts are my forte.

SOCRATES: Did you ever live among these proletarians whose lives you describe so strikingly?

MARX: I do not need to come to them; they come to me.

SOCRATES: Have they come to you? How many proletarians have joined your Communist Party in all the years of your life? How many proletarian friends do you have? Or even acquaintances? Could you even tell me the full name of a single proletarian person?

MARX: What a ridiculous question! Of course.

SOCRATES: I'm waiting.

MARX: Lenchen.

SOCRATES: Ah, yes, that peasant woman your family kept as a slave without ever paying her a cent in wages. You are right: you do have some experience of exploitation.

MARX: What do you know about Lenchen?

SOCRATES: I know that you had your will with her not only financially but also sexually. I know that you refused to acknowledge as your own son the boy you fathered by her; that you refused to meet him and forbade him to be seen by your rich and influential friends at the front door, so that he could only visit his mother in the back kitchen.

MARX: You are a liar, Socrates!

SOCRATES: We neither can nor need to argue about this, Karl, for you know the truth.

MARX: I call you a liar for claiming you are here to judge my book, not my soul.

SOCRATES: I do not know your soul. But I do know your life. And your life illuminates your book, so it is rightly part of my investigation.

But we must return to your book itself. You write,

Society can no longer live under this bourgeoisie. . . . The essential condition for the existence, and for the sway of the bourgeois class, is the formation and augmentation of capital; the condition for capital is wage labour. Wage labour rests exclusively on

competition between the labourers. The ad-
vance of industry, whose involuntary pro-
moter is the bourgeoisie, replaces the isola-
tion of the labourers, due to competition, by
their revolutionary combination, due to as-
sociation. The development of Modern Industry, therefore, cuts from under its feet the
very foundation on which the bourgeoisie
produces and appropriates products. What
the bourgeoisie, therefore, produces, above
all, is its own grave-diggers. Its fall and the
victory of the proletariat are equally inevitable.

MARX: I am rather proud of that paragraph, if I do
say so myself.

SOCRATES: And justly so. I certainly compliment you
on the power of your writing. You combine here an
extended logical argument with memorable rhetoric.

MARX: But you wonder whether it's all *true*.

SOCRATES: You are getting to know me well. Yes, that
is what I wonder. Because behind the rhetoric is a
very important claim: that you have discovered the
mechanism by which the machine works, the machine of social history.

MARX: So now you want to try to falsify my claims
by some empirical observations and perhaps some
statistics, is that it?

SOCRATES: No, I want to take a shorter route: I want
to test your claim by the law of non-contradiction.

MARX: There is no contradiction in that paragraph,
I assure you.

SOCRATES: Perhaps there is a contradiction between something in it and something outside it: your act of writing it.

MARX: What do you mean?

SOCRATES: Do we write books to try to persuade the parts of a machine to do the work it must do with mechanical necessity? Have you ever read a *Gear Shift Manifesto*?

MARX: No. But it was you who used the image of the machine, not I. I prefer a biological analogy. I have discovered the mechanism by which society evolves, as Darwin discovered the mechanism by which species evolve.

SOCRATES: But with equal necessity.

MARX: Yes.

SOCRATES: Well, do we write books to persuade natural selection to get on with its work? Have you ever read an *Amphibian Manifesto*?

MARX: This is silly, Socrates.

SOCRATES: Yes, but I think it is your silliness, not mine. But let us further test what I think. Tell me, please, do we try to persuade triangles to keep their three sides? Do we exhort two apples to continue to be half of four apples? Do we argue with the rain to make it fall, or with the body to persuade it to grow old?

MARX: Of course not.

SOCRATES: Why not?

MARX: Because such argument is unnecessary.

SOCRATES: And why is such argument unnecessary?

MARX: Because the things themselves are necessary.

SOCRATES: I think you are exactly right. They are all inevitable rather than freely chosen. But now you say that the proletarian revolution is also inevitable and necessary. And you do not believe there exists any such thing as free will or free choice. So why, then, do you write your book to try to persuade the proletariat to do that which, according to your book, the proletariat cannot help doing? Why preach to the machine?

MARX: Because even though it is inevitable, it needs causes. It will necessarily happen, but it will happen through necessary causes. And one of those causes is my book. I do not need to introduce anything from free will. I am an instrument of destiny, of history.

SOCRATES: I see. Your act of writing the book is necessary.

MARX: Yes.

SOCRATES: And what is necessary is not a free choice of the will?

MARX: Correct.

SOCRATES: Therefore your act of writing is not the free choice of your mind or will.

MARX: That's right. As I explain in chapter 2:

the theoretical conclusions of the Communists are in no way based on ideas or principles that have been invented, or discovered, by this or that would-be universal reformer. They merely express, in general terms, ac-

tual relations springing from an existing class struggle, from a historical movement going on under our very eyes.

SOCRATES: So you can't help how your tongue happens to wag or how your pen moves.

MARX: Or even how my brain thinks.

SOCRATES: So the thoughts in this book of yours are just as necessary, as unfree, as the thoughts that come to an insane man because a piece of bone is pressing on part of his brain.

MARX: Yes, indeed. All things have causes that are necessary and material, and that law applies to thoughts as well.

SOCRATES: Both sane and insane thoughts.

MARX: Yes.

SOCRATES: Then why should anyone pay any attention to yours and not to those of the lunatic?

MARX: Because mine are scientific, and therefore they explain and account for everything.

SOCRATES: Except, perhaps, for their own author. But we will bring this up again later.

10

Private Property

MARX: Socrates, is it really your purpose to examine my book fairly?

SOCRATES: Indeed it is.

MARX: Then you ought to follow its topics and order more carefully rather than continually going off onto your philosophical, idealistic tangents about free will and mind and self.

SOCRATES: They are not tangents, nor are they particularly *mine*. I do not compel the argument to follow me, but I do compel myself to follow the argument. But you are right in saying that we must be more conscientious in following the topics and the order of your book. So let us look at the relation between chapter 1 and chapter 2. Chapter 1, "**Bourgeois and Proletarians**", is about the past and about the problem. Chapter 2, "**Proletarians and Communists**", is about the future and about the solution. Is that a fair outline?

MARX: It is short but accurate. And in chapter 2 I demolish every objection to Communism. So you as a philosopher should like this chapter, since you like arguments.

SOCRATES: I like arguments only as I like maps: they are means to an end. The end is the finding of truth.

Nevertheless, I am happy that you who do not share my end will at least share my means, argument.

MARX: Why do you say I do not share your end?

SOCRATES: You yourself say it. You explicitly say that the end of Communism is power, not truth: **"The immediate aim of the Communists is . . . formation of the proletariat into a class, overthrow of the bourgeois supremacy, conquest of political power by the proletariat."**

MARX: But of course our aim is power: we Communists are doing politics, not philosophy. Politics is about power. What else could it be?

SOCRATES: Here is what else it could be. Politics could be about justice, about true justice. Might could be put into the hands of right instead of right being determined by might. That is the classical alternative to your system.

MARX: Oh, you mean the idealistic philosophy made famous by your disciple Plato in his *Republic*, the illusion Machiavelli refuted once and for all.

SOCRATES: Did he, now? Some time I must tell you about the conversation I had here with him. But in any case you do use arguments in this chapter, and I am happy to examine them.

MARX: Please do. You spend as much time saying what you're going to do as doing it. I knew you philosophers preferred thinking to acting; I didn't realize there was something you preferred even to thinking.

SOCRATES: What is that?

MARX: Thinking about thinking.

SOCRATES: Touché. Congratulations, Karl, you are beginning to develop a sense of humor. The air in this country does wonderful things to the mind.

MARX: Can we get down to business, please?

SOCRATES: Touché again. Well, in this chapter you attempt to answer, not quite "every" objection to Communism, as you said a moment ago, but the nine that are probably the most serious and common. And all of the objections are put in the same form: the objector claims that Communism is not a plus but a minus; that it destroys rather than creates, or takes away rather than gives, nine precious things for mankind: private property, individuality, motivation for work, culture, the family, private education, monogamy, nations, and finally religion and philosophy.

MARX: That is correct. And you will note that I order them in a hierarchy, with the most important one first and the least important one last. Thus I say **"the theory of the Communists may be summed up in a single sentence: Abolition of private property."** You idealists have it exactly upside down.

SOCRATES: How silly of us to think more of truth than of money! Well, we will follow your order and investigate its basis later. We will begin, as you do, with the argument about property.

You first formulate your objector's objection. (By the way, this is a technique you rarely use in your writing; you seem to have an aversion to dialogue.) Then you give your reply. The objection is this:

We Communists have been reproached with the desire of abolishing the right of personally acquiring property as the fruit of a man's own labour, which property is alleged to be the ground work of all personal freedom, activity and independence.

And your reply is this:

Hard-won, self-acquired, self-earned property! Do you mean the property of the petty artisan and of the small peasant, a form of property that preceded the bourgeois form? There is no need to abolish that; the development of industry has to a great extent already destroyed it, and is still destroying it daily.

Or do you mean modern bourgeois private property?

But does wage labour create any property for the labourer? Not a bit. It creates capital, i.e., that kind of property which exploits wage labour, and which cannot increase except upon condition of begetting a new supply of wage labour for fresh exploitation. Property, in its present form, is based on the antagonism of capital and wage labour. . . .

You are horrified at our intending to do away with private property. But in your existing society, private property is already done away with for nine-tenths of the population; its existence for the few is solely due to its non-existence in the hands of those nine-tenths. You reproach us, therefore, with intending to do away with a form of prop-

erty the necessary condition for whose existence is the non-existence of any property
for the immense majority of society.

In one word, you reproach us with intending to do away with your property. Precisely so; that is just what we intend.

That is truly great rhetoric, Karl. Let us see whether
it is also convincing to the reason.

The objection could be summarized as follows, I
think: Communism abolishes private property. But
private property is a good thing. Therefore Communism abolishes a good thing. But whatever abolishes a good thing is a bad thing. Therefore Communism is a bad thing.

The argument is logically valid, so if you want to
answer it, you must find either a false premise or an
ambiguous term. And you do agree with its first
premise—that Communism abolishes private property—but not with its conclusion—that Communism
is a bad thing. Is this correct?

MARX: Yes. And the ambiguous term is "property".
That's the logical point of my answer to the objection, in that long passage that you quoted. Bourgeois
Capitalism has already abolished *feudal* property, the
kind the bourgeoisie idealizes. Communism does not
abolish that; *Capitalism* does. Communism abolishes
bourgeois property.

SOCRATES: I see. And you say that this bourgeois
property *ought* to be abolished, that it is a bad thing
rather than a good thing. (The second premise of my
summary of the objection had claimed that it is a
good thing.) And you also give a reason for what you
say: that it is a bad thing because it exists for the .

owners only at the expense of the workers. Is my analysis correct so far?

MARX: Yes.

SOCRATES: Then why is that bad? Why is it a bad thing if the masses are denied property so that the owners can amass it?

MARX: Are you playing with me?

SOCRATES: Not at all.

MARX: Then are you implying that a society ruled by robber barons is a good one?

SOCRATES: No, I am only asking for your reason for thinking that it is a bad one.

MARX: But no one denies that that is a bad thing. The Capitalists do not deny that premise; they only deny that that bad thing is being done under Capitalism.

SOCRATES: Then, if Capitalists and Communists agree about that, *why* do they agree that it is a bad thing? What is their reason?

MARX: Why, because it is exploitation and oppression, of course. It is an imposition of power on the weak by the strong.

SOCRATES: And why is *that* bad?

MARX: That is a silly question. No one ever asks it. There is no disagreement that it is bad.

SOCRATES: But there may be a disagreement about *why* it is a bad thing.

MARX: What disagreement do you have in mind?

SOCRATES: Well, some, like myself, would say that it is bad because it is unjust. Is that what you say?

MARX: I do not believe in some transcendent, universal, unchangeable Form or essence of justice, as you do. I believe that ideas are only the products of societies, of their class structures and modes of production. And these things change as history's dialectic unfolds. From these two premises it follows that the validity of all ideas changes, that there is no realm of unchanging universal truths, such as a "justice", that could be a common standard for comparing and judging different societies, different eras, and different classes.

SOCRATES: I thought so. So you would not say it is bad because it is simply unjust.

MARX: No.

SOCRATES: But you do call it bad.

MARX: Yes.

SOCRATES: For no reason or for some reason?

MARX: For good reason.

SOCRATES: Then I wonder what your reason is.

MARX: It does not further the revolution.

SOCRATES: But why is the revolution good?

MARX: Because it issues in the classless society.

SOCRATES: And why is that good?

MARX: Because it ends oppression and class warfare.

SOCRATES: And are those things bad?

MARX: Yes—by Communist standards. But not by the standards of the classes that are the winners. This is what you do not understand, Socrates: that our ideas of good and bad are thoroughly relative to our era in history and to our social class.

SOCRATES: This is our deepest philosophical difference, I think.

MARX: It is our deepest *philosophical* difference, but philosophical differences cannot be the deepest differences. And that is itself our deepest philosophical difference: about the status of philosophy, about the status of ideas.

SOCRATES: You mean you do not think much of philosophy.

MARX: I mean that I am a realist, and you are an idealist.

SOCRATES: That is how we are usually classified. But what, exactly, do you mean by those two terms?

MARX: I believe that real events cause ideas; you believe ideas cause real events.

SOCRATES: I believe that thinking is a real event. Don't you?

MARX: Here, let me play Socrates to you for a minute. Do you agree that the criteria or standards by which we judge real events are ideas?

SOCRATES: Yes: they are ideas about what is really good and bad.

MARX: Now suppose you have a student—let's call him Plato—who you thought was your friend. And suppose that he one day enters your house and robs you of all your money. Would you not change your idea about him and no longer think he is your friend but your enemy?

SOCRATES: That is difficult for me to imagine.

MARX: Why, because you have such trust in Plato?

SOCRATES: No, because I never had any money to steal.

MARX: Seriously, Socrates, imagine it, just for the sake of the argument.

SOCRATES: Some say that actually happened to me, in the realm of ideas rather than money. May I use that scenario instead?

MARX: No! My whole point is about the impotence of ideas and the power of things like money. Ach, what am I doing? You are probably the last person in the world I could ever hope to persuade of *that*. Look here, all I need you to admit is that your ideas about a person would change because of the different way that person acted.

SOCRATES: That is true, of course, and I will admit it.

MARX: Then don't you see? The point is simple: our ideas are the products of real events, not causes of them.

SOCRATES: By "real" events you mean only material events, not events like thinking.

MARX: Yes, unless you will admit that thinking, too, is a material event.

SOCRATES: I will not admit that it is a merely material event.

MARX: You are diverting me from my argument!

SOCRATES: I am only answering your questions.

MARX: Do you admit that ideas are products of material events?

SOCRATES: Certainly. The example of the thief shows that.

MARX: Well, then, so-called master of logic, don't you see the logical implications of that admission? You should be a materialist, like me, not an idealist.

SOCRATES: But I also believe that material events are products of mental events; that a man moves his arm because he thinks he should move his arm. Do you deny this ever happens?

MARX: You keep diverting me onto this metaphysical issue no matter what we begin with!

SOCRATES: I thought it was the logic of the argument itself that did that. But suppose it was I and not the argument that diverted you. Why should I not do this?

MARX: Because you are supposed to be examining my book, and my book is not about any of your favorite subjects, such as supposedly objective, universal, and unchangeable essences like man and mind and justice and truth. It is about power and wealth and history and class conflict.

SOCRATES: So it is unfair of me to change the subject.

MARX: Yes.

SOCRATES: And do you mean by "unfair" roughly the same thing you mean by "unjust"?

MARX: I suppose so.

SOCRATES: So you are appealing to justice to criticize me for thinking about justice.

MARX: I am impatient with all this abstract logical swordplay.

SOCRATES: That tells us something about your likes and dislikes but nothing about the nature of reality outside your likes and dislikes.

MARX: Then let me tell you something about the nature of reality, if you will be patient enough to listen.

SOCRATES: I have been waiting patiently for just that.

MARX: Not only justice but human nature itself is malleable. That is why human justice changes. There is feudal justice, and there is bourgeois Capitalist justice, and there is proletarian Communist justice, and they are incompatible. What is justice to one is injustice to another. And private property is the prime example. All the bourgeoisie call it unjust that under Communism property is public; and all Communists call it unjust that under bourgeois Capitalism property is private and that it accumulates among the bourgeoisie at the expense of the proletariat.

You see, Socrates, justice is a class concept: not an abstract *logical* class concept, a *genus*—there is no such thing as generic justice—but a *social* class concept. Capitalist justice is bourgeois justice; Communist justice is proletarian justice.

SOCRATES: I see: by your account each social class seeks its own self-interest and calls that "just", and that is all there is to justice.

MARX: Exactly. Now you see it, Socrates.

SOCRATES: But I do not see, then, what is the difference between justice and self-interest or between justice and selfishness or between justice and power?

MARX: Why must there be any difference at all, in the last analysis?

SOCRATES: Because we have two different words here, "justice" and "power", which we use very differently. If they meant the same thing, we would not need two words but only one. But we have two, because we all—even you—judge some uses of power to be just and others to be unjust; we judge power by justice. And we try to form and limit selfishness and self-interest by this other thing that we call justice. At least the vast majority of mankind do, in every time and place and culture and social class. But you seem to disagree with them. You seem to say that there is no such thing as justice; that it is only another word for power or class interest—only another *word*, not another *thing*.

MARX: I agree that this is where we differ: you think justice is a real thing, and I do not. But how do you propose to find out whether it is a thing or only a word? It's all abstract argument, with no empirical facts to disprove the arguments, so we are like birds flying through the empty air.

SOCRATES: I propose that we begin by knowing what we are arguing about. We must have some concept of justice in order to affirm that it exists, and we must have some concept of it to affirm that it does not exist. So what is this concept that the masses believe is a thing and you believe is a mere word?

MARX: That's precisely our difference, Socrates: I say it is a mere concept, a ghost, a fancy, a fantasy, not a real thing.

SOCRATES: But I did not ask for its status in reality; I asked for its meaning. I asked for its essence, and you told me its existence (or non-existence, according to you). But even if you are right and it is a mere fantasy, we need to know *what* this thing is that is a mere fantasy.

MARX: I refuse to waste my time and thought on word games such as you and Plato played.

SOCRATES: In other words, you will not or cannot answer my question.

MARX: What I can and will do is to insist that you return to the data, to what I have written in my *Manifesto* in answer to the objection about property.

SOCRATES: Gladly. The objector says that Communism is bad because it destroys private property, which is good. And your answer is that Communism does *not* destroy private property; Capitalism has already done that. So Capitalism is the villain. Is that a fair summary?

MARX: Put in your terms, yes. Communism only destroys "bad" private property, that is, Capitalist property, bourgeois property. So what don't you understand about that?

SOCRATES: This: If Capitalism has destroyed something good, why not restore that something good? Why join with the Capitalists in opposing the whole pre-industrial medieval order even more vehemently than Capitalism does, if that order is good? And if that order is bad, then Capitalism is not the villain but the hero for destroying it.

MARX: Again you assume unchanging, absolute standards of good and bad, Socrates. I deny your assumption. Your whole logic is based on those "eternal forms" of yours, which simply do not exist.

SOCRATES: So you refuse to comply with simple logical requests like "Define your terms" or "Prove that you do not contradict yourself" because you do not believe there is anything unchanging, even in logic?

MARX: I did not say that. I can do formal logic as well as you can, just as I can do math.

SOCRATES: Then please answer my question: What is the ambiguous term or the false premise or the logical fallacy in the argument against Communism that you are answering here?

MARX: I've already told you: the ambiguous term is "property". The historical dialectic produces, not some one unchanging eternal form called "property", but many different and incompatible forms of property, many different things that are all called by the same name. And I say the same about "good" and "bad": they are historically relative. What is good at one stage, because it serves the march of history, is bad at another stage, because it retards it. As a man passes through the same intermediate level of seawater as he sinks to the bottom to drown and again as he rises to the top to be rescued: on his way down, it is regress; on his way up, it is progress.

SOCRATES: So Capitalism is like that intermediate level of seawater.

MARX: Yes. It is good in serving history's purpose by paving the way for Communism; and it is bad in being the last obstacle to a worldwide Communist order.

You see, here is the root error of you idealists and absolutists. Even when you do not speak about God, you endow your own ideas with Godlike attributes. You keep assuming the existence of some immaterial, perfect, ideal, timeless, unchanging standard of goodness or justice—something outside history and above it, sitting in judgment of it like a God. So you are his prophets; you judge each changing age and society by the same unchanging standard. But I say your standards are nothing but your prejudices produced in you by the changing forms of your society. Real, concrete social changes are the causes of your ideas. Societies produce these ideas in the minds of their citizens. Social changes cause ideas rather than ideas causing social changes.

SOCRATES: I congratulate you for identifying the key philosophical point of difference between us—between all you materialists, whether Communist or not, and all ordinary people: you think the trees move the wind while we think the wind moves the trees.

MARX: I don't follow your metaphor. Both wind and trees are material things. We differ about how matter and thought are related, not about how two pieces of matter are related.

SOCRATES: I am sorry: I forgot how literalistic you materialists tend to be. I meant the trees as symbols for all visible, material things and the wind as a symbol for the invisible things, spiritual things, like ideas and choices.

MARX: Then you are using an argument from analogy, and that is a logical fallacy.

SOCRATES: My analogy is not meant to prove anything but to illumine. It is not an argument but an explanation.

MARX: Well, it fails. It misleads. You may call us literalists, but we materialists are scientific, and you idealists are not.

SOCRATES: Why do you think this is so?

MARX: Because science has discovered the material causes of mind. Scientifically speaking, the human mind is insignificant.

SOCRATES: How can that be? Scientifically speaking, the human mind is the scientist!

MARX: Abstract wordplay! I prefer to be concrete instead. That is why I say that no matter what the individual is, mind or matter, the individual is insignificant, historically speaking.

SOCRATES: But, historically speaking, the individual is the historian!

MARX: You are very good at rhetoric, Socrates.

SOCRATES: No, I am not. That is not rhetoric, that is logic.

MARX: Call it what you will. I appeal to facts, not logic. You may serve logic, but I serve history. And history's winners and losers are not determined by who has the more logical arguments. My philosophy will win as a historical fact. I care not whether it wins in this little game you call dialogue or argument.

SOCRATES: Then why argue at all? Why not use guns instead?

MARX: Are there any here?

SOCRATES: No. You must use arguments. They are your only weapons here.

MARX: I will use them. But I will not serve them.

SOCRATES: Why do you use them?

MARX: To move some men at some times, "the pen is mightier than the sword."

SOCRATES: So it is power over men that is your end.

MARX: I am a politician, Socrates, not a philosopher.

SOCRATES: I take that as a "Yes". Do you seek power for its own sake, then, or as a means in the service of something higher, like justice?

MARX: I have told you already, Socrates: there is no such thing as some generic, universal justice.

SOCRATES: And you say the same about truth as about justice.

MARX: I do. It changes with history.

SOCRATES: So there are no changeless and universal truths?

MARX: No.

SOCRATES: So all truths change?

MARX: Yes.

SOCRATES: Is *that* truth a changeless and universal truth?

MARX: I tire of your pretty logic games, Socrates.

SOCRATES: You tell me about your feelings, but you do not tell me about facts. Is this what you mean by being scientific?

MARX: We know facts with our senses, Socrates, not with abstract ideas and arguments.

SOCRATES: But that principle is itself an idea, or an argument.

MARX: Let me put it very simply: I am an empiricist. We know only what we see. The rest is speculation.

SOCRATES: "See", with our senses?

MARX: Yes.

SOCRATES: But we do not see *that* with our senses. For *that* is not a *thing*, with color, or an *event*, with movement in space. It is an idea, a belief, a proposition. No one can *see* it. So if you are right in saying that we know only what we see, then we do not know *that*.

MARX: Socrates, I thought your purpose here was to examine my book.

SOCRATES: It is.

MARX: We haven't quoted it for a long time.

SOCRATES: Nevertheless, we have not forgotten it. We are exploring its two covers, so to speak: its assumptions and its implications, its foundations and its consequences.

MARX: Well, let's explore *it* instead. Why must we fight on your ground instead of mine?

SOCRATES: For one thing, because we are not fighting. For another, because although your book may be yours, the laws of logical reasoning are not yours any more than they are mine. They are like the laws of physics or geometry or arithmetic. But yes, we should return to your book.

11

Objections to Communism

SOCRATES: The next seven objections to Communism that you list, and your answers to them, all seem to fall into the same logical pattern. So let us consider all seven objections together. Here is a summary of what you wrote:

[Objection 2] **"You say, individuality vanishes [under Communism].**

[Reply] **"You must . . . confess that by "individual" you mean no other person than the bourgeois, than the middle-class owner of property. This person must, indeed, be swept out of the way and made impossible. . . .**

[Objection 3] **It has been objected that upon the abolition of private property all work will cease, and universal laziness will overtake us.**

[Reply] **According to this, bourgeois society ought long ago to have gone to the dogs through sheer idleness; for those of its members who work, acquire nothing, and those who acquire anything, do not work. . . .**

[Objection 4] **Objections . . . have . . . been urged against the Communistic modes of producing and appropriating intellectual** products. Just as, to the bourgeois, the disappearance of class property is the disappearance of production itself, so the disappearance of class culture is to him identical with the disappearance of all culture.

[Reply] That culture, the loss of which he laments, is, for the enormous majority, a mere training to act as a machine.

But don't wrangle with us so long as you apply, to our intended abolition of bourgeois property, the standard of your bourgeois notions of freedom, culture, law, etc. Your very ideas are but the outgrowth of the conditions of your bourgeois production and bourgeois property, just as your jurisprudence is but the will of your class made into a law for all, a will whose essential character and direction are determined by the economic conditions of existence of your class. . . .

[Objection 5] **Abolition of the family! Even the most radical flare up at this infamous proposal of the Communists.**

[Reply] **On what foundation is the present family, the bourgeois family, based? On capital, on private gain. In its completely developed form this family exists only among the bourgeoisie. But this state of things finds its complement in the practical absence of the family among the proletarians, and in public prostitution.**

The bourgeois family will vanish as a matter of course when its complement vanishes,

and both will vanish with the vanishing of capital.

Do you charge us with wanting to stop the exploitation of children by their parents? To this crime we plead guilty.

[Objection 6] But, you will say, we destroy the most hallowed of relations when we replace home education by social.

[Reply] And your education! Is not that also social, and determined by the social conditions under which you educate, by the intervention, direct or indirect, of society, by means of schools, etc.? The Communists have not invented the intervention of society in education; they do but seek to alter the character of that intervention, and to rescue education from the influence of the ruling class.

The bourgeois clap-trap about the family and education, about the hallowed co-relation of parent and child, becomes all the more disgusting, the more, by the action of Modern Industry, all family ties among the proletarians are torn asunder, and their children transformed into simple articles of commerce and instruments of labour.

[Objection 7] But you Communists would introduce community of women, screams the whole bourgeoisie in chorus.

[Reply] The bourgeois sees in his wife a mere instrument of production. He hears that the instruments of production are to be exploited in common, and, naturally, can come to no other conclusion than that the lot of being common to all will likewise fall to the women. . . .

The Communists have no need to introduce community of women; it has existed almost from time immemorial.

Our bourgeois, not content with having the wives and daughters of their proletarians at their disposal, not to speak of common prostitutes, take the greatest pleasure in seducing each other's wives.

Bourgeois marriage is in reality a system of wives in common and thus, at the most, what the Communists might possibly be reproached with, is that they desire to introduce, in substitution for a hypocritically concealed, an openly legalized community of women. . . .

[Objection 8] The Communists are further reproached with desiring to abolish countries and nationality.

[Reply] The working men have no country. We cannot take from them what they have not got.

There! I trust that was a long enough excerpt to quench your thirst for written data for a while. Now I see the same logical pattern in each of these objections. The objection says that Communism is bad because it abolishes something good: property, individuality, work, culture, families, home education, monogamy, and nations. And I see the same logical pattern in each of your replies: that it is Capitalism, not Communism, that has already done this abolishing. Is my analysis correct so far?

MARX: Yes.

SOCRATES: So in each case you do not deny the factual point the objector makes in each objection: that under Communism none of these things will be allowed to exist.

MARX: Not in its old form.

SOCRATES: But you deny the point about value, the objector's evaluation of the fact. You shift the blame for the damage from Communism to Capitalism, as a child, accused of fighting, might answer, "But he started it!" But you continue the same fight even more radically, do you not? Like a child accused of lighting fires with a match, you point to another child's matches, and then you turn on your own blowtorch.

MARX: Your childish insults do not matter; what I say is true.

SOCRATES: My point is not that you lack truth but that you lack logic. The logical form of all your replies is the fallacy logicians call *tu quoque* ("you too", in Latin).

MARX: Explain, please.

SOCRATES: To use an analogy from war or sports, you substitute an offense for a defense. Or, to use a term from the psychologists, you use "transference". It is the need to blame your accuser for what he catches you doing.

MARX: But he *is* doing it!

SOCRATES: Perhaps he is. But what you say reveals more about you than about him. You seem to be much happier to prove that your accuser is wrong than that you are right; happier to admit that you both did evil than that you both did good. The evil of Capitalism seems so much more important to you than the good of Communism that you do not even try to answer the charge that Communism is evil! All you do is try to show that Capitalism is evil too. Now I'm not a psychologist, but it seems pretty obvious, even to me, that you have an obsession with your enemy, or with your own consuming hatred for it.

MARX: It deserves to be hated! If there were a God, he would hate it, too!

SOCRATES: So you see yourself as the prophet of this—this cold and wrathful God?

MARX: You have read my poems, haven't you?

SOCRATES: Indeed I have. I found the language very powerful and arresting. Especially in the *Savage Songs* you published in 1841, where you call us humans **"the apes of a cold God"**, and where you say **"I shall howl gigantic curses at mankind."**

MARX: Thank you for being perceptive to the power in them.

SOCRATES: I was also perceptive, I think, to the hatred and misanthropy in them. You frequently quoted with approval the devil's line from *Faust*, "Everything that exists deserves to perish." In fact, most of your writings thrive on catastrophe, violence, apocalypse, pacts with the devil, and suicide. If you had lived in the twentieth century, I think you would rejoice at the sight of a fireball of destruction incinerating a whole city or a suicide mission blowing up the world's tallest buildings. And I think I see something even worse, something I do not see in many others who would also rejoice at such destruction: that you do *not* rejoice at the sight of a mother nursing a baby or of a loving, contented, happy private family in their own home enjoying each other's company and the simple pleasures of nature.

MARX: What low-class, disgusting claptrap you throw in my face, Socrates! You are truly a bourgeois idiot, fondling in your mind these images of nursing babies and mothers while the old world is burning and changing forever.

SOCRATES: You are no longer in that old world, Karl.

MARX: What world do you mean?

SOCRATES: The world that was full of families and nature, the world that was created by your Enemy.

MARX: The bourgeoisie killed that old world, not I.

SOCRATES: They did not. It will still exist, centuries later, when your fever dreams have died, after having taken millions of lives down with them.

MARX: Tell me more about the future.

SOCRATES: I will tell you this much, Karl: that in the long run your ideas are responsible for more deaths, more destruction, more murders, more misery, more mayhem than those of any other thinker or writer who has ever lived.

MARX: History has assigned this destiny to me: to be the prophet of the apocalypse! You know, in my original version of *The German Ideology* I prophesied a Day of Judgment, **"when the reflections of burning cities are seen in the heavens . . . when the 'heavenly harmonies' consist of the melodies of the *Marseillaise* and the *Carmagnole*, to the accompaniment of thundering cannon, while the guillotine beats time and the inflamed masses scream *Ça ira, ça ira*, and self-consciousness is hanged on the lamp-post."**

SOCRATES: I must congratulate you: that is one of the most powerful descriptions of the mind of Hell that the world has ever seen. I thought the last line especially profound.

MARX: You overstep your bounds, cruel ironist. You were supposed to examine my book, like a man, not my soul, like a god. What do you think you are?

SOCRATES: It was my lifelong task to find out. Perhaps I did overstep the boundaries of my task as a philosopher. But every philosopher is a man before he is a philosopher. As for overstepping the bounds by pretending to be a God of judgment—that is precisely my accusation against you. And in that accusation all I did was read your words and praise them for their power.

MARX: You cannot judge my soul.

SOCRATES: Indeed not—especially if you do not have one, as you claim in your philosophy. But I can judge your published words. That is not overstepping my bounds.

MARX: You left my book halfway through. You left seven good arguments hanging in midair.

SOCRATES: I will return to them now.

MARX: Why? What motivates you?

SOCRATES: The desire to help you to know yourself.

MARX: What if I do not accompany you on that road?

SOCRATES: That choice is no longer open to you.

MARX: What? Why not?

SOCRATES: Because you are dead.

MARX: Where am I, then?

SOCRATES: You are in the place where self-consciousness cannot be hanged on the lamppost.

12

Individuality

SOCRATES: We must complete our analysis of your little book. No important stone can be left unturned here, no matter what creatures crawl out from under it.

We have explored the first objection, about private property. The second is about individuality. In reply to the objection that Communism abolishes individuality, you say two things: first, that it only abolishes *bourgeois* individuality and, second, that the bourgeoisie have already abolished individuality.

MARX: Yes. And that is not a contradiction, as you are probably going to say it is, because "individuality" is not one thing but many. It is what you logicians call "equivocal".

SOCRATES: Do you mean that there is nothing common to both bourgeois individuality and Communist individuality?

MARX: That is exactly what I mean.

SOCRATES: Nothing at all?

MARX: Nothing at all. You are surprised by that, Socrates, only because you still think of everything in terms of that old, prescientific superstition called "nature" or "the nature of things" or things having "essences", or "species" as being objectively real. I call that the illusion of "species-being". I am a nominalist, like most modern philosophers, and also a historical relativist. And so I tell you that "species" are nothing but concepts artificially constructed by the mind—that is, by the mind-set produced by different eras and different class systems—that is my nominalism—and that these systems change radically according to the dialectic of history—that is my historical relativism.

That is the great divide between us, Socrates. You prescientific, romantic, idealistic, traditional, religious thinkers stand on the old side, the dying side, the side that desperately grasps ghosts and spirits and tries to keep them from withering away. We progressive, scientific thinkers stand on the other side, the side that is coming to birth. We are freed from your ghosts, whether God or gods or souls or species. "Species" are only Aristotle's weakened form of Plato's "eternal Ideas", which in turn were only Plato's weakened form of the old gods.

SOCRATES: You accept Auguste Comte's three-stage theory of history, then: an upward progress from "the religious" to "the philosophical" to "the positive-scientific".

MARX: In ideas, yes. But ideas themselves are only the shadows cast by real material events. Your disciple Plato was as wrong as he could possibly be in his famous allegory of the cave. I turned Plato inside out.

SOCRATES: Most historians say you turned Hegel upside down. But it goes back farther than Hegel, back to Plato.

MARX: When will we return to my text, please? It seems that no matter what specific issue we explore, we keep coming back to this general philosophical issue about ideas.

SOCRATES: That is because they are connected. For instance, how can we return to the "specific" topic of individuality if there are no such things as "species"?

MARX: Clever wordplay, Socrates. A mask over your failure to understand me.

SOCRATES: Then let me try again. When you talk about "individuality", you deny that there is any one meaning to it, do you not?—I mean, that there is any universal and unchanging nature or species or "whatness" of this thing that we call human individuality that does not change through time, at least not in its substance or essence, even while its accidental qualities are changing. Do I understand you rightly so far?

MARX: Yes—if you also understand the reason for my position. It is because human individuality is not determined by nature, as is the human circulatory system, for instance. It is not the product of biology, of evolution. It is the product of thought, which itself is the product of class structure and social changes, which are rooted in economic changes.

   This is why I answer the bourgeois objection that says "Communism abolishes individuality" by saying that it does indeed, but it only abolishes *bourgeois* individuality. You see, private ownership of property has already created an entirely different kind of individuality for the bourgeoisie than for the individual under the old feudal system; and Communism will create still another, entirely different, individuality by abolishing private property and private ownership.

SOCRATES: I see. If the cause of individuality is economics, then to change the economics is to change the individuality.

MARX: That's exactly it. So you *do* understand my point.

SOCRATES: I think so. To put it more simply, if we grow up in a Capitalist society, we learn to say "me" only when we learn to say "mine", and we learn to say "mine" only when we possess something we can call "mine", that is, private property.

MARX: I couldn't have put it better myself.

SOCRATES: No, I don't think you could. So there *is* no Cartesian "I think, therefore I am"—no innate, natural, private, mental self-consciousness.

MARX: Exactly! That is what I meant by **"hanging self-consciousness on the lamp-post"**. You understand the logic of my argument now.

SOCRATES: Yes, but I do not understand what you mean by individuality under Communism.

MARX: Of course you don't; you are irredeemably bourgeois.

SOCRATES: Let me try. In your all-Communist world, would no one say "I" any more, but only "we"? Is that what you mean? If that is the advertisement for your Heaven, I am surprised you think many people will buy it, for it looks more like what most people would mean by Hell.

MARX: Again, you say that because you have a bourgeois mind. You would not say that if you were a proletarian. The proles have nothing to lose, and they have a world to win.

SOCRATES: But—to quote a very famous economist —what does it profit a man to win the whole world and lose his own self?

MARX: You old moralists have it all backward again. The self is the product of the world, not vice versa. Self-consciousness is determined by economics, not vice versa. Thought is the effect of matter, not vice versa.

SOCRATES: Again we come to this crucial idea, your materialism. But it is you as a thinker who thinks that idea and who approves that idea and who proves that idea—the idea that thought is the effect only of matter, not of mind. So it seems that your thought disproves itself. It destroys its own credentials.

MARX: I don't see why.

SOCRATES: If thoughts are nothing but the necessary effects of the blind bumping around of mindless atoms, why should anyone listen to the words that came out of your mouth because of that particular bumping around of atoms in your brain rather than someone else's? Or to the thoughts caused by material events that happened when you wrote your *Manifesto* rather than the ones that happened when you were a baby or when you were drunk?

MARX: Because some are true and others are false, of course.

SOCRATES: But if what you say is true, then all thoughts, both true ones and false ones, are equally material.

MARX: Correct.

SOCRATES: And there is no *material* difference between true ones and false ones. The brain of the man who speaks the truth is not bigger or rounder or grayer than the brain of the man who speaks falsehood. We cannot tell which one speaks truth by how loud his voice is.

MARX: I don't see your point.

SOCRATES: Why should anyone listen to that particular wave on the sea of matter called Marx rather than to another called Socrates?

MARX: We do not freely choose to listen to one particular wave on the sea of matter. All is determined, both the waves and the listening. History chooses us; we do not choose history. And the image of the wave is a good one, for a wave is not as individual as it looks. The individuality of a wave is an illusion. And so is the individuality of the bourgeoisie.

SOCRATES: Who, then, is victimized by this illusion of individuality, if not some real individual? And if there is no particular individual, how is it that you, Karl Marx, and not another man, refutes the illusion of individuality by which others are victimized? Do you not see the irony here? You deny the reality of your own I, of the very I with which you deny your own reality! You deny the I and worship the We, and yet it is the I, the lonely I, who does this.

MARX: Such individualistic and so-called "inner" arguments do not move me.

SOCRATES: Then I will use a social and external argument. You worship the We and deny the I, yet the We, society, the masses—yes, even the proletariat—believe in the I and not in your philosophy that denies the I for the We. Only a few elite individuals, only the educated, the alienated, the uprooted, believe you. The masses are superstitious peasants, religious traditionalists, conservative old fogies like me. They fear your revolution.

MARX: That's because they don't know what's good for them. That's why they need my book, and why I write it.

SOCRATES: Do you know why they fear your revolution?

MARX: Of course: because they are conservative.

SOCRATES: And do you know why they are conservative?

MARX: Because they are stupid.

SOCRATES: No, because they are happy.

MARX: That is utter nonsense.

SOCRATES: Let us see. Why are they called "conservatives"?

MARX: Because they oppose change.

SOCRATES: And why do they oppose change?

MARX: Because they want to conserve the old order.

SOCRATES: Right. Now do we want to conserve things that make us happy or things that make us unhappy?

MARX: Happy.

SOCRATES: And do we want to change things that make us happy, or things that make us unhappy?

MARX: Unhappy.

SOCRATES: Therefore conservatives are, by definition, happy. They are conservative *because* they are happy. And radicals are, by definition, unhappy. They are radicals *because* they are unhappy. In fact, some of them are so miserable that they just want to destroy everything in sight and write apocalyptic words like "everything that exists deserves to perish."

MARX: That is a clever argument, Socrates, but it is like a dream. It is powerless. It exists wholly within the confines of your abstract logic and has nothing to do with history and the real world. You may have won the argument, but I will win the world. Thought is your master, but history is mine. And I do not fear your master.

SOCRATES: Well, I hope you fear yours. For history is a god that consumes its worshippers.

13

Can Human Nature Be Changed?

SOCRATES: We must now consider your answer to the next objection, that Communism abolishes the motivation to work, since it abolishes the motive of competition, the motive of attaining excellence, the motive of being better than others.

MARX: This issue is really about what you call "justice", I think. Communist justice is very different from bourgeois justice. It does not need or encourage competition. There are no losers under Communism. Its formula for justice is this: **"from each according to his ability to each according to his need"**, as I said in my *Critique of the Gotha Program*.

SOCRATES: That sounds very high-minded. But I want to see exactly what it means, concretely. I think a homely example best tests a high-minded principle, so since I know more about teaching than about economics, let me take an example from the world I know best. Suppose I were a teacher who was giving my students a test and grading them. I would say that it would be just to give each individual what he deserves. So I would treat equals equally and unequals unequally. I would not give the same grade to good work and to bad work. That is my "bourgeois" concept of justice. And it fosters competition—competition with oneself, at least, and competition against failure. Now suppose that I were to practice Communist justice as a teacher instead. I suppose that would mean that I would collect all my students' work and give a grade to each, then calculate the class average, and then give that same grade to every student, so that all would share equally and there would be no losers and no competition. Now do you really think that students would work as hard in the Communist class as in the other class? Isn't it human nature to be lazy unless we are rewarded or punished?

MARX: You forget, Socrates: there is no such thing as "human nature". Bourgeois students under a Communist teacher would not work. But Communist students would, just as bourgeois students work under bourgeois teachers.

SOCRATES: So you are going to change human nature.

MARX: Certainly.

SOCRATES: It would be a radical change, indeed. For I have never seen anyone—any individual or any family—take less care of his own private property than of public property. They do not clean the toilets at City Hall first, before their own, or mow the grass in the public park more carefully than the grass in their own yard. What will cause them to change their strong instinct to put the private first?

MARX: Again, you have it backward, Socrates. The instinct was created by private property, and it will be removed by removing its cause.

SOCRATES: Do you think that people will simply stop desiring private property just because it has been taken away from them?

MARX: No, not those who still remember having it and long to return to their drug. But their children will; the next generation will. We will eradicate old memories. We will master the past as well as the future.

SOCRATES: So you will turn selfish egotists into selfless saints just by changing the economy?

MARX: If the economic cause is powerful enough to change the self itself, individuality itself, then it is surely powerful enough to change the consequences of individuality, such as whether the motivation to work requires private property or not.

SOCRATES: So the answer is "Yes".

MARX: Yes.

SOCRATES: You will create a greater difference in human nature than anyone has ever done before, a greater difference than Christ or Buddha.

MARX: Of course. Why do you mention them?

SOCRATES: Because they also claim to change human nature itself.

MARX: And why do you say my claim is greater than theirs?

SOCRATES: Because even they do not claim to produce in this world what you claim to produce: a society of selfless, sinless social saints.

MARX: My case rests.

SOCRATES: The effect is truly impressive, but let us look at its cause. The cause that you say is powerful enough to produce this radical effect, this revolution, this new man—it must be truly tremendous. Greater than the causes Buddha and Jesus appealed to, for they have not yet brought about the perfect society of selfless saints that you promise. Buddhism appealed to the "Noble Eightfold Path" to bring about the abolition of all desires, which in turn would bring about Nirvana-consciousness, perfect bliss. And Christianity appealed to the miracle of God becoming man and dying and rising to conquer sin and death to bring about salvation, or a "new birth", the possession of man's soul by the Holy Spirit. But neither Buddhism nor Christianity has produced a whole society of selfless saints. So your cause must be truly awesomely great if it is able to bring about a greater change than these two ever did.

MARX: Their religions only *claimed* to cause changes.

SOCRATES: Like yours.

MARX: Ah, but history will deliver my product.

SOCRATES: Alas, your prophecy is true. It will. But the product will not be what you think.

MARX: And the reason it will work while religion does not is because religion appeals to man's free choice. Communism will not rely on such a weak foundation.

SOCRATES: Alas, again you prophesy truly. In any case, what is this all-powerful cause that will finally do what nothing else has ever done?

MARX: You are toying with me, Socrates. You know my answer to that question. It is Communism.

SOCRATES: Which is essentially a new economic system, the abolition of private property.

MARX: Yes.

SOCRATES: So all we have to do to effect that change is to remove the obstacle of private property.

MARX: Yes.

SOCRATES: By taking away the money and property of the bourgeoisie.

MARX: Yes.

SOCRATES: Against their will, of course.

MARX: Of course.

SOCRATES: So the great cause of this transformation from sinners into saints turns out to be *theft*.

MARX: That is what the bourgeoisie would call it. But that assumes that private property is good. I assume it is evil. What you call theft, I call salvation.

SOCRATES: Then why was the transformation not accomplished before? History certainly has seen a lot of theft—excuse me, a lot of "salvation".

MARX: History has seen only transfers of power and property from one private person to another, or from a few to a few.

SOCRATES: So theft on a grand scale, global theft, will accomplish what petty theft could not?

MARX: Your bourgeois sarcasm does not change the facts, Socrates. What you call "theft" is destined to produce equality and justice forever.

SOCRATES: I think I have heard that argument before: "the end justifies the means"; "let us do evil so that good may come"; "it is expedient to kill one innocent man for the sake of the people."

MARX: What's your point, Socrates?

SOCRATES: Only that I now see your point, I think, and how very different Communist "justice" is from the ordinary idea of it. But—forgive me—I have once again wandered far from my task of examining your text. It is time to consider the next objection.

14

Communist Culture: An Oxymoron?

SOCRATES: Your next objection and reply is about culture. You were indeed prophetic here, for in the century after yours, when Communism held sway over half the world, the culture it produced would be remarkable in two ways. First, despite the enormous numbers, not a single orthodox Communist was ever a writer, artist, or musician of the first magnitude . . .

MARX: By bourgeois standards, of course.

SOCRATES: However, Communism would produce many great writers and artists and musicians, all as protesters, as dissidents, as heroic haters of Communism and sufferers under Communism, many as martyrs under Communism. But not a single one as a lover of Communism.

MARX: I foresaw this objection in my answer. And my answer was that bourgeois Capitalism has already destroyed culture, but **"that culture, the loss of which he laments, is, for the enormous majority, a mere training to act as a machine."**

SOCRATES: This is how you would describe Dickens, Blake, Wordsworth, Coleridge, Pope, Tennyson, Goethe, Cézanne, Milton, Emerson, Rembrandt,

Monet, Tchaikovsky, Beethoven, Mozart, Dostoyev-
sky, Tolstoy . . .

MARX: What's your point, Socrates?

SOCRATES: That you see all these artists as merely
the agents of a culture that is "a mere training to act
as a machine"—while Communist culture is *not*?

MARX: That is what I maintain, exactly.

SOCRATES: You are serious, aren't you?

MARX: Again I say: What's your point, Socrates?

SOCRATES: Perhaps my point should be praise to
your prophetic powers again. A century or so after
you died, the technique you use here would be made
famous by a master of propaganda who would call it
"The Big Lie". His point was that little lies are easily refuted and seen through, but a truly big one of-
ten stuns you into acceptance of it.

But we must look at your argument instead of trad-
ing insults.

MARX: I'm still waiting.

SOCRATES: Your argument here seems to be nothing
new, only the same argument that you use to answer
every objection. You say that the objector is only ap-
plying his bourgeois notions to Communist things,
but **"your very ideas are but the outgrowth of the**
[material] **conditions of your bourgeois production and bourgeois property"**—in other words,
money determines *everything*, even ideas, and economics is the queen of the sciences, as theology used
to be.

MARX: Back to the same issue again.

SOCRATES: And in this passage you also clearly deny any such thing as justice and reduce it to propaganda for force: **"just as your jurisprudence is** [nothing] **but the will of your class made into a law for all."**

MARX: But this is not personal, individual force. It is the force of history. I am no Machiavelli. (What are you muttering under your breath, Socrates?) No, it is the will of a class, not of an individual. And even that is only the inevitable result of material things: **"a will whose essential character and direction are determined by the economic conditions of existence of your class."**

SOCRATES: Well, it seems that we have clarified your position but not proved it or disproved it. We have proved only that you do really mean what you say. And perhaps that is the most important point for the average person investigating your thought: to see clearly, to understand what Communism is, so that no evasions or nuancings can camouflage it. For most people, no argument will be necessary; seeing will be enough.

15

The Family

SOCRATES: We now come to your next point, Communism's call for the abolition of the family. Here even more than before, I think that understanding rather than argument is enough; that merely seeing that you are serious and mean what you say will be quite sufficient for the great majority of people, especially for those to whom you appeal, the proletariat, the poor.

Perhaps I should begin by praising you for your logical consistency. You perceive that the family and religion and a self, or a soul, and what you call the bourgeois sense of individuality stand or fall together.

Your answer to the objection that Communism abolishes the family begins by asserting that **"the present family, the bourgeois family,** [is based] **on capital, on private gain."** Thus you believe that it will disappear once its cause disappears. Is that correct?

MARX: Yes.

SOCRATES: And its cause is—capital!

MARX: It is.

SOCRATES: Do you really believe what you write, that the bourgeois husband **"sees in his wife a mere instrument of production"**?

MARX: Would I have written it if I didn't believe it?

SOCRATES: I don't know; would you?

MARX: Let's just say that what I have written, I have written.

SOCRATES: That saying sounds familiar. I wonder— never mind. Tell me, did you formulate the principles of Communism before or after you met the woman you married?

MARX: After.

SOCRATES: So before that, you were not a Communist.

MARX: True.

SOCRATES: What kind of society did you grow up in? A feudal society?

MARX: A bourgeois society.

SOCRATES: So you were one of the bourgeoisie, then?

MARX: Yes.

SOCRATES: So as a bourgeois, when you proposed to your wife, you said something like this?—"O Jenny, will you consent to be my instrument of production?"

MARX: Sarcasm is not logic, Socrates.

SOCRATES: Will you answer my question?

MARX: I thought you knew everything here.

SOCRATES: My goodness, no. Only you and Jenny know the answer to that question. And she arrived here years ago and has passed on to a much higher and brighter place than you could possibly endure.

MARX: My point is just that the bourgeois family is based on oppression.

SOCRATES: Of women or of children?

MARX: Both.

SOCRATES: And does your own experience confirm that judgment?

MARX: I grew up in an oppressive family, yes.

SOCRATES: And did you in turn oppress your wife and children? As all bourgeois fathers do, according to your theory?

MARX: Unfair, unfair!

SOCRATES: But if Jenny were here, I'm sure she would confirm your theory. And so would "Little Fly" and Franziska. But they have passed on, too. And Freddy is not due for years.

MARX: How do you know about Henry Frederick?

SOCRATES: Engels told Tussy before he died, in 1895, that Freddy was your bastard son.

MARX: So Eleanor knows? Engels told my Eleanor? The traitor! But how can you know the future?

SOCRATES: All time is present here.

MARX: This is simply intolerable. I will not endure it! Whoever is behind you, you imitation-Socrates, I will annihilate you and them!

SOCRATES: You now look exactly like the man Bruno Bauer's brother described: "In fury raging, his evil fist is clenched, he roars interminably, as though ten thousand devils had him by the hair." Or, even better, you look like Karl Heinzen's description of you:

"a cross between a cat and an ape . . . spitting out spurts of wicked fire." Or Lassalle . . .

MARX: Lassalle was an utter fool. You must take my description of him first and in its light evaluate his description of me.

SOCRATES: If you insist. In a letter to Engels (July 30, 1862), you described your friend, Germany's first great labor leader, as **"the Jewish Nigger"** and **"a greasy Jew disguised under brilliantine and cheap jewels. As the shape of his head . . . indicates, he is descended from the Negroes who joined in Moses' flight from Egypt (unless his mother or grandmother on the father's side was crossed with a nigger)."**

MARX: What's your point?

SOCRATES: Just that your readers can decide for themselves whether you are the man they can trust to replace the institution of the family with some radically new substitute of your own devising.

MARX: I will abolish the exploitation of children by their parents!

SOCRATES: You would do that, indeed. And you would do it by abolishing children and parents! It is like abolishing a disease by abolishing all those suffering from it. I must admit that it does seem to be 100 percent effective. But at a 100 percent cost. So, by your economics, is that cost-effective?

MARX: Yes, it is! For the State will be the universal family, the universal parent, and the universal children, since the State will be the people and the people will be the State.

SOCRATES: I see: with the abolition of private property comes the abolition of the private family, since a wife and children are nothing but property.

MARX: Under Capitalism, yes.

SOCRATES: And privacy itself will disappear once its economic cause, private property, is abolished.

MARX: The bourgeois form of it, yes. The Communist form will be wholly different.

SOCRATES: Your contemporaries already know what the bourgeois form of it is, from their present and from experience. But they cannot know anything of the Communist form yet, until it becomes present rather than future. Until then it is not experienced data but mere "idea"—a category you seem to scorn, yet here you rely on the idea to displace the reality. And surely the future itself is only an idea at the present time, while the present and the past are both real data and fact, in the most concrete, material, and scientific ways. Yet you would destroy the present and the past for the sake of your dreamed-of future. I think you are the very idealist you criticize!

MARX: I thought for a moment that you understood me.

SOCRATES: I think I understand you only too well.

16

Education

SOCRATES: Your next objection and reply concern education. It follows the same logical pattern: shifting the blame to your accuser while remaining ambiguous about whether the crime is to be praised or blamed. What is to be abolished by Communism is home education, or private education. I presume you would include in this category not only home schooling but also all privately-controlled, privately financed educational institutions and that under Communism you would replace them all with a single State-controlled education. Is that correct?

MARX: Yes. But under Communism the State will eventually be indistinguishable from the people, from society, after a brief transition period during which the State must centralize power for the war on the bourgeoisie . . .

SOCRATES: By the way, will that war be political or military?

MARX: It will be economic, and the means to it will be political.

SOCRATES: And suppose it does not succeed at the ballot box?

MARX: Communists are not pacifists, Socrates. In countries that are not democracies we must use other than democratic means to seize power. That is obvious.

SOCRATES: And these means are military.

MARX: We candidly confess this. The revolution will be bloody.

SOCRATES: In other words, as a means to your success, you intend to kill a very large number of people. Thank you for clearing up that point.

MARX: But after the State withers away—

SOCRATES: Why will it wither away, by the way?

MARX: To fulfill its destiny, like a woman's placenta after she has given birth. It is history's dialectic.

SOCRATES: Tell me, who administers a State?

MARX: Men administer it, of course. But they are only the instruments of a higher power.

SOCRATES: And do men have wills?

MARX: Of course, but they are not free.

SOCRATES: And are those wills material or spiritual?

MARX: Material.

SOCRATES: And can two material bodies occupy the same place at the same time?

MARX: No.

SOCRATES: So they are inevitably in competition.

MARX: Yes, so far. But under Communism—

SOCRATES: Let us confine ourselves to our data for now. The law of all material things is the law of division, or subtraction, is it not? If two men share a pie or a fortune or a physical space, each one loses whatever part the other one gains.

MARX: Yes. That is why the abolition of private property is so radical . . .

SOCRATES: But when a teacher shares his wisdom with a student or a man shares his love with his wife or an artist shares his creativity with his audience, are they diminished? Or are they multiplied or added?

MARX: What's your point, Socrates?

SOCRATES: That matter and spirit follow opposite laws and that when we observe some things not following the laws of matter, we can conclude that they are not material things.

MARX: I thought you were talking about the State withering away under Communism. Again you slip into metaphysics.

SOCRATES: I will slip back into politics.

MARX: And what's your point there?

SOCRATES: That a State is run by men, and men have wills, and those wills are selfish because according to you they are material. So what will motivate these selfish men to sacrifice their power and "wither away"?

MARX: I did not use that phrase in print, by the way. But it is a good one. They will wither away as a leaf does in the fall, because its time has come. The moving force of history is not individual wills, Socrates, but collective destiny. You keep looking at everything from your bourgeois, individualistic perspective.

SOCRATES: So "destiny" will suddenly turn selfish, power-hungry thieves and violent killers into self-sacrificing saints. Those who believe in an omnipotent God say that not even he can perform that miracle against our free will; that is why there exists a Hell. Perhaps you are more religious, more pious, more submissive to the omnipotent will of your god than any Jew or Christian or Muslim is.

MARX: What outrageous things you say, Socrates!

SOCRATES: I am sorry that you are outraged instead of refuted, or refuting. It seems we have degenerated into insult rather than logical argument. And again I have diverted us from your text. That is why it is good to have a text in front of you when you have a long and deep discussion of it with many tangents: it gives you a home to return to. So let us return.

You want to remove private education. Your opponent objects to this. And your answer to him is that Capitalism has already done this damage. You say that all education is in fact social but that under Capitalism its agent is neither individuals nor families, as the bourgeoisie claim, nor society as a whole, nor the State, as it will be under Communism, but the bourgeoisie as a class. Is that a fair summary?

MARX: Yes. You can be quite logical when you try, Socrates, as well as sarcastic. You know, I could really use you in my cause, if you should ever change your mind.

SOCRATES: You could indeed, but not as your servant but as your teacher. I would never answer an objection with a sneer and a spitting.

MARX: When did I do that?

SOCRATES: Right here in the text: **"The bourgeois clap-trap about the family and education, about the hallowed co-relation of parent and child, becomes all the more disgusting. . . ."** You reveal much about your own subjective feeling and deep hatreds here, but little about objective reality.

MARX: But I do! I am angry at bourgeois hypocrisy.

SOCRATES: Where is their hypocrisy?

MARX: In self-righteously defending families and children in their words when in their lives those families and children are being oppressed and exploited.

SOCRATES: Where? How?

MARX: In all Capitalist countries, in industrialized countries all over Europe. In factories.

SOCRATES: Especially in England, where you did your research every day sitting in the British Museum?

MARX: Yes.

SOCRATES: As an empiricist and not an idealist, you must have made many trips to actual factories to gather your data. Of course, if you were only an idealist, you would have kept your nose in a book all day. But if you were scientific, you would have looked for, and accounted for, data that counted *against* your theory, too, such as factory reform laws produced by Capitalism.

MARX: They prove nothing. Or else they prove the existence of massive oppression that they tried feebly to correct.

SOCRATES: They prove that bourgeois Capitalist societies were capable of correcting their own abuses and oppressions.

MARX: That's a matter of argument.

SOCRATES: Then let us look at a matter of data. Can you list or count the times you actually set foot inside one of these factories that you claim are the centers and agents of Capitalism's certain self-destruction?

I seem to hear a deafening silence. Even Engels toured one English factory once and invited you to come, but you would not. Isn't that so?

And could you point me to one single passage in all your writings where you confront, not your enemy's *arguments*, as you do in this chapter of the *Manifesto* that we are exploring, but rather his *data*?

Hmm . . . I must be getting deaf. I do not hear your answer. Or perhaps I am deaf to what *you* mean by "scientific".

17

Women

MARX: You are becoming more sarcastic and less philosophical, Socrates.

SOCRATES: Does that make you happy or unhappy?

MARX: Why would it make me happy?

SOCRATES: Because if I am becoming sarcastic and unphilosophical I am becoming more like you and less like me.

MARX: It makes me unhappy because you are in control here.

SOCRATES: Oh, no. You are.

MARX: What?

SOCRATES: Whenever you give me a reason to be philosophical or irenic or objective, I am. When you give me a reason to be sarcastic, I am that. I am a mirror. My task is only to reflect, to enlighten, to help you to know yourself.

And so we must continue along the road your book has cut for us. The next objection concerns your replacement for the family: community of women (and, presumably, children—for effective contraception had not yet been invented in your day).

MARX: It is a replacement for the *private* family. What you bourgeois minds call simply "the family" is only one of the many forms it can take.

SOCRATES: So you would not object to a family without a father or with many fathers or many mothers or two or more homosexual "parents"?

MARX: I would welcome these as I would welcome all revolutions, even if they are not fully Communistic. They are steps. They are destabilizing.

SOCRATES: You mean they eliminate the enemy.

MARX: They accomplish the ground-clearing for the new building, the new society. They help the snake slough off his old skin. They help free the moth from the chrysalis, the baby bird from the egg. You have to crack an egg to hatch a bird.

SOCRATES: You mean they eliminate the enemy.

MARX: If the egg resists being cracked, the egg becomes the baby bird's enemy.

SOCRATES: Does anything material *not* resist being cracked?

MARX: No, not the smallest atom. But when it is cracked, who knows what energy might not be released?

SOCRATES: No one, indeed. And you would destroy the old order, which we know, an order that all admit to be a mixture of good and bad, for the sake of a new order about which no one knows with certainty how good or bad it will be because no one has ever seen it.

MARX: They see it in my books.

SOCRATES: You are an empiricist, are you not?

MARX: Yes.

SOCRATES: As an empiricist you must agree that knowing is dependent on seeing.

MARX: Yes.

SOCRATES: But you have only thought, and not seen, your new order.

MARX: So far.

SOCRATES: And you would destroy the order that is seen for the sake of the order that is unseen. You would destroy people and families and many lives and happiness for the sake of an idea.

MARX: What's your point, Socrates?

SOCRATES: I think you are a hidden idealist.

MARX: I am a hammer opening the egg of history.

SOCRATES: The new bird that would emerge from this egg, the new energy that would be released by destroying the atom, or the atom of the family—who knows whether this unknown genie you would release from the bottle will be good or bad?

MARX: I do not claim to know everything with certainty. But I have hope that man can be better, far better, than we have seen.

SOCRATES: Then your revolutionary fervor must be motivated by hatred of man as he is rather than by love of man as he could be; for only man as he is, is real and knowable—unless you are a radical idealist, like my student Plato. He, too, called for the abolition of the family, and also of private property, in his picture of an ideal society in his *Republic*, but not for the whole society but only for a tiny ruling class, which he thought of as a serving class, like priests in the Catholic Church. He was much less radical than you.

MARX: I, too, moderate my radicalism, though not by numbers, as Plato did, but by time. The revolution will take place in steps. It may take a generation or two before some societies will be ready for the completion of the task of replacing the bourgeois family.

SOCRATES: But eventually, you hope and work for "community of women" worldwide?

MARX: Yes. *All* women must be liberated.

SOCRATES: From husbands.

MARX: From bourgeois, private husbands.

SOCRATES: And children from parents.

MARX: From bourgeois, private parents.

SOCRATES: And will Communist women have no husbands, and Communist children no parents?

MARX: No. Everyone will belong to everyone.

SOCRATES: Sexually as well?

MARX: How could privacy be abolished if private sexual control is not abolished?

SOCRATES: I see. You think of sex as *control*.

MARX: Certainly.

SOCRATES: No wonder you had such difficulty experiencing sexual happiness. No, don't bother shaking your fist at me. I know that was a low blow. I'm sorry. I have this obsession with truth; I wrongly assume that the truth of what is said excuses any impoliteness and impropriety. I apologize for the personal insult. But not for the question. For the questions that arise about your radically new social order seem like a large herd of elephants.

MARX: I haven't worked out all the details yet.

SOCRATES: I think that will not be a very reassuring response to the person who sees elephants coming.

MARX: I gave an answer to the objection in my *Manifesto*, you know.

SOCRATES: Do you? Excuse me. I must have missed it. Where?

MARX: In the very words on that page, you sarcastic swine!

SOCRATES: You mean these words? **"The Communists have no need to introduce community of women; it has existed from time immemorial."**

MARX: Yes.

SOCRATES: Well, if this is your answer, let us examine the evidence for it truth. Do you say that adultery is the norm in the most primitive societies?

MARX: Yes.

SOCRATES: And by the "norm" you mean, not a moral ideal, but a habitual social practice?

MARX: Yes.

SOCRATES: And how prevalent would you say this habit must be to make it the norm?

MARX: Oh, let's say eight or nine out of ten cases.

SOCRATES: So you say that 80 percent of men in primitive societies were unfaithful.

MARX: That sounds like a reasonable figure.

SOCRATES: And in ancient Rome? And in medieval Christendom?

MARX: The same, in all likelihood.

SOCRATES: Then, since effective contraception was unknown, very many children must have been illegitimate, in fact, the great majority.

MARX: That follows. But it is easy to cover that up.

SOCRATES: Here, indeed, we have some empirical data, though only one example.

MARX: What do you mean?

SOCRATES: I mean that here, finally, you do speak from experience.

MARX: You are a cad, Socrates.

SOCRATES: I am a mirror. Nothing can be hid for long here. So you say that in bourgeois society—for instance, the Victorian England you lived in for a time—husbands were no more faithful than they were in primitive tribes?

MARX: Probably. Who knows?

SOCRATES: *You* seem to know. Isn't that what you wrote, in effect?

Our bourgeois, not content with having the wives and daughters of their proletarians at their disposal, not to speak of common prostitutes, take the greatest pleasure in seducing each other's wives. Bourgeois marriage is in reality a system of wives in common and thus, at the most, what the Communists might possibly be reproached with, is that they desire to introduce, in substitution for a hypocritically concealed, an openly legalized community of women.

MARX: Let it be so. Stet!

SOCRATES: Would you like to know the exact figures? We are excellent statisticians here.

MARX: No. Let's get on with my book.

SOCRATES: That is exactly what I thought we were doing.

MARX: Next question, please.

SOCRATES: I will exercise mercy instead of justice and do just that, since my inquisition has caused you to sweat rather distressfully. By the way, we also have very good soaps, showers, and perfumes here if you would care to alter your appearance a bit.

MARX: What's the catch?

SOCRATES: Only that there can be no conflict here between appearance and reality, so you would have to embrace a corresponding inward washing, which so far I have not been very successful in even beginning to convince you to embrace.

MARX: I shall retain my own clothes and personality, thank you. Can we get on to the next question, please?

SOCRATES: Here it is, then: Why do you not speak of a "community of men", but only a **"community of women"** under Communism?

MARX: There is total equality between the sexes under Communism.

SOCRATES: I see. So if you were a good Communist and not a hypocritical one, you would be just as happy about your Jenny's affair with Engels as you are about your affair with Lenchen.

MARX: Engels? Engels! Et tu, Brute? I will annihilate him! That jakesnipe, that jackal, that greasy Jew!

SOCRATES: I must stop this experiment quickly. I cannot endure the smell.

MARX: Experiment? What do you mean?

SOCRATES: I mean that Engels had no such affair, but we now can all see, from your response to my question, just how happy you would be in your own Communist Utopia.

MARX: You slimy bourgeois sneak! You—you lawyer! You said you could not lie here.

SOCRATES: I did not say Jenny's affair with Engels was real. I raised the flag of the thought—the thought of the very equality between men and women that you claim to preach—but you did not salute it.

MARX: A dirty trick!

SOCRATES: A trick, yes. The mirror uses tricks of sudden light. But the dirt it reveals comes only from the man in front of it. Would you like a little soap now? It's free, you know.

MARX: I'd prefer a little gun. Are they free here, too?

SOCRATES: No weapons can exist in this place. And its mirrors cannot be broken.

MARX: This is unendurable!

SOCRATES: I truly hope that is not your last word on the subject. For if it is, I have failed. For if that is your last word, then that will be your last word.

MARX: I don't understand.

SOCRATES: Good! Therein is your hope. And my opportunity—to help you to understand.

MARX: I do not understand that, either.

SOCRATES: Good; you are learning Lesson One.

MARX: Is there any point in going on?

SOCRATES: Yes.

MARX: It is hopeless.

SOCRATES: It is your only hope.

MARX: Then go on. I have no choice—or do I? Is there another place? Another road I can take out of here?

SOCRATES: There is no other place for now and no other road. You must walk the very road you made in life. No one can walk another's road. You can choose only to walk or not to walk.

MARX: And suppose I choose the "not"?

SOCRATES: You have already chosen to walk, however reluctantly; that is why you are here, with me, in the place of hope. Your road is extremely long and hard and slow, but you are on it, so there is hope. Shall we proceed, then?

MARX: Proceed.

18

Nations

SOCRATES: The next objection is hardly worth mentioning, for it follows exactly the same pattern. It is that **"Communists are further reproached with desiring to abolish countries and nationality."** And your reply is that **"the working men have no country. We cannot take from them what they have not got."**

Again it is not clear whether you say Capitalism is bad because it has stolen from the proletariat a thing that is good—nations—or that Capitalism is good because nations are bad, and it has destroyed this bad thing.

It is also far from clear that your premise is true: working men are usually more patriotic, not less, than the richer and more educated classes.

And it is also unclear whether your future one world order, minus individual nations, will be better or worse than the old order, with nations. Like families, nations are things that nearly everyone agrees have produced both good and bad. And to exchange an imperfect but known good for something wholly unknown would seem to be motivated, as before, more by hatred of the real thing that is known than by love of the ideal thing that is unknown. (Unknown unless, of course, you are an idealist instead of an empiricist.) For how can we love what we do not know?

And if we do know it, we know it only as an idea, for it is not yet real. Thus again you rank idea over reality. You are an idealist, not a realist.

But these questions are not new; they are the questions we have already asked about nearly every controversial issue you have raised. And they have not been answered.

What *is* new, and basic, is your last point, the last of the nine objections, the one about ideas and ideology, philosophy and religion. So I would like to move on to that, unless you want to add something about the issue of nations.

MARX: I do. It is a very simple point: One world would mean no war.

SOCRATES: Yes. But if nations are good things, would that not be like killing the patient to cure the disease? Or like amputating a limb to cure a hangnail?

MARX: Sometimes only radical treatments cure. Nothing else has ever eliminated wars. For as long as there are nations, there will be nationalism, and as long as there is nationalism, there will be war.

SOCRATES: And as long as there are individual egos, there will be egotism. So the only cure for egotism and selfishness and oppression is to eliminate its cause . . .

MARX: So you *do* see my point.

SOCRATES: . . . by eliminating the "I" itself and replacing it with the "we".

MARX: Yes, that's it.

SOCRATES: So this whole business we are now engaged in, this "know thyself", is quite superfluous if you *have* no self.

MARX: Very good. May I go now?

SOCRATES: Who is the "I" who is asking to go?

MARX: Are you toying with me again?

SOCRATES: I am. And at the same time, I am in deadly earnest. And I wonder whether a "we" can ever be deadly serious.

MARX: Why not?

SOCRATES: Because if there is no "I" and no family and no nation and no conflict and no war, then what is the "other"? If there is only one "we" throughout the world and forever, if "we are the world", then what can "we" possibly do that matters, that makes a difference?

MARX: Are you defending war?

SOCRATES: No, but I am defending its possibility.

MARX: What do you mean by that?

SOCRATES: Nations, and love of one's nation, seem rather like one's family and one's self. All three easily fall into diseases of egotism. But your surgery for all three seems to be euthanasia.

MARX: Everything has its time to die, Socrates. Even those three things.

SOCRATES: Everything except Communism?

MARX: Communism will live forever. It will outlive nations and families and bourgeois individuality.

SOCRATES: You are due for some surprises.

19

Three Philosophies of Man

SOCRATES: The last objection that you consider, the one concerning philosophy, is for you the least important.

MARX: That's why I put it last.

SOCRATES: Yet you spend more time answering it than any other, except the first, the one about private property.

MARX: That is because most people, like you, and most philosophers, and certainly all idealists have everything upside down; and they must be answered.

SOCRATES: Here, then, is the crucial passage—philosophically, the most important passage in your book. For this choice is the most basic and foundational and makes the greatest difference to the greatest number of things.

MARX: I disagree. I think it makes no difference at all, except in thought. The issue of the status of ideas is important only if you begin from the idealist's assumption that thought causes things rather than vice versa. But from the materialist point of view it is last, not first—in power and in importance.

SOCRATES: What are ideas, then, according to your ideas? Could we say that since they are not made of matter, they do not matter?

MARX: I do not deny their reality altogether, so don't bother trotting out your clever logical objections against that position, that it is self-contradictory. I account for ideas by real material things. Ideas are effects, but not causes. And they are not observable phenomena, only epiphenomena.

SOCRATES: Those are the two points summarized in the term "epiphenomenalism", the term philosophers have given to your position about the status of ideas. What do you mean by saying that they are not causes of real events?

MARX: Ideas accompany real events, as spectators might accompany a military battle, to observe it. But they do not affect the outcome of the battle. The phenomena are the real things. They are material and therefore observable. Epiphenomena sit on top of phenomena. "Epi" is the Greek prefix for "on top of". Epiphenomena are like clouds floating on top of the events that take place on the surface of the earth. They are like the heat generated by electricity running along a wire to a machine. The electricity does all the work and causes the machine to work. That is the electricity's product, or effect. But it also generates a by-product: the heat you can feel in the wire. But the heat simply dissipates into the air. It does not affect the machine. Ideas are something like that heat, and matter is like the electricity. Do you know about machines and electricity, Socrates? You did not have them in your world, and you do not seem to have them in this world.

SOCRATES: I know about everything in your life.

MARX: Then consider the difference between a steam engine and another machine that generates steam as a by-product. In a steam engine it is the steam that effects the work. In other machines, steam is simply discharged into the air through tubes or smokestacks. The immediate or proximate cause of the steam of our ideas is the brain. The ultimate cause, or first cause, of these ideas is our socio-economic system, the class structure of society. This shapes our thoughts as well as our actions.

SOCRATES: In other words, the money system.

MARX: In the broad sense, yes.

SOCRATES: So if you want to find the First Cause, follow the money trail. That is, indeed, a new path to God.

MARX: The first cause is matter, not God. Just as the cause of our thoughts is our brains, not some spirit or ghost called "mind".

SOCRATES: Do you say that our thoughts are discharges from our brains?

MARX: You may say that.

SOCRATES: Perhaps we could call this "the cerebral flatulence theory of consciousness."

MARX: Call it what you will, it is what science discovers.

SOCRATES: I thought that science discovered data. Do you say it discovers theories?

MARX: It discovers that the brain is full of chemicals and physical nerves, rather like little wires, and that when you touch a certain nerve with a piece of electrically charged metal or suffuse it with certain chemicals, you can produce or modify a certain thought or feeling. When you alter the chemicals, you alter the consciousness. That's data.

SOCRATES: That is true. And when you bump a writer's pen, you change the message.

MARX: What does that analogy prove?

SOCRATES: No analogy proves anything. Analogies only show or illustrate. And this one shows that the data you mention could also be explained by another theory: that the brain is the *instrument* of thinking rather than the *cause* of thinking; that there is a mind or soul or spirit or self that uses the body and its brain, as a writer uses a pen. The data are compatible with both hypotheses, yours and mine.

MARX: Not so. I challenge you: Name me one single act of thinking or feeling or anything else that you claim is immaterial—mystical experience, even, or falling in love or moral compunction or mathematical calculation—and I will find a scientist who can find exactly what part of the brain, or what chemical change in the brain, is its cause. Cut out one part of the brain, and a man cannot feel pain. Cut out another part, and he cannot reason. Cut out a third part, and he no longer makes moral choices. You can perform a consciencectomy. There is not a single datum to prove anything immaterial, not a single act of your so-called soul that cannot be explained by some observable, material event in the body, especially the brain.

SOCRATES: That is an impressive argument, and a real one, for it is based on real data; and it deserves to be answered.

MARX: I'm waiting.

SOCRATES: You have drawn up two columns, each with a long list of items. Column One is matter, or body, or brain. Column Two is spirit, or soul, or mind. And you say there is no item that falls under Column Two that cannot be explained by a corresponding item in Column One, so Column Two is superfluous, a mere copy or ghost image of Column One. Is that correct?

MARX: Yes. But the argument is stronger than that. Each corresponding item in Column One, each physical or chemical part or state or act of the brain, can also be shown to be the *cause* of its corresponding mental event. For when you prod one part of the brain with a piece of metal or an electrical charge or a chemical, you make a man see purple; and when you prod another, you make him afraid; and when you cut out a little piece of the brain matter, a man can no longer count up to ten. These are facts, and you cannot argue with facts.

SOCRATES: But I can argue with your theory. It is not the only one that accounts for all the facts. There are, in fact, three theories that account for all these facts, I think.

MARX: I doubt that, but what are they?

SOCRATES: One of them is a theory neither of us believes: that matter does not exist, that all is mind. If

I believed this theory, I would then challenge you with exactly the same argument you gave to me, but in reverse.

First, I would challenge you to produce a single item in Column One, a single so-called material thing or event, that has no corresponding mental event, no item in Column Two. You could never do it, because the very act of thinking, or expressing your thinking, *is* the corresponding mental event or idea. If the idea does *not* correspond to the thing, it is not a true idea, not an idea of that thing.

Second, I would say that the argument is even stronger, for I can show causality as well as correspondence. For when you take away a man's thought of anything, no evidence of that thing remains, just as when you remove the dreamer, you remove all evidence of the dream.

I know you can explain the same data in the opposite way. But my point is that the immaterialist can, too. And so can I, for I believe a third theory: I am a dualist: I believe both columns are real, both mind and matter. And I believe that these two things interact in us; each can influence the other, in different ways. Or perhaps their relation is better expressed this way: They are two dimensions of one person that cannot be reduced to one, somewhat like the syllables of a poem and the meaning of the poem.

The point is simply that all three theories explain the data. For there is always a correspondence between the two columns, and when one item is removed, its corresponding item also disappears.

MARX: So what is your "bottom line"? Where does all this argument leave us?

SOCRATES: Ready, finally, to read the argument in your book.

20

Materialism

SOCRATES: You write: **"The charges against Communism made from a religious, a philosophical, and, generally, from an ideological standpoint, are not deserving of serious examination."**

This is a very clever debater's trick: When you have no answer to your opponent's strongest objection, use insult instead. The "snow job" might cow him. It's the preacher's trick: "point weak here, holler like Hell."

MARX: But I *do* answer the objection. Read on.

SOCRATES: **"Does it require deep intuition to comprehend that man's ideas, views and conceptions, in one word, man's consciousness, changes with every change in the conditions of his material existence, in his social relations and in his social life?"**

I could answer your rhetorical question on its own level by saying that it does *not* require deep intuition; it requires shallow intuition. It requires confusion.

For you can mean two very different things by this sentence. First, you can mean simply that whenever there is some change in the material world that we are aware of—for instance, the change from night to day, or from a kiss on the face to a slap on the face—there is also a corresponding change in our consciousness. That, indeed, does not require deep intuition to comprehend, and it is true, and everyone admits it, the idealist as well as the materialist. It proves nothing. It certainly does not prove materialism. Material changes produce corresponding mental changes simply because thought *observes* these material changes, and if any thought is to be true, it must correspond to reality, including material reality. We dualists believe that no less than you materialists do.

So I think you must mean a second thing by that sentence I quoted from you. You must mean that material social conditions are *the sole and sufficient causes*, and thoughts are *merely their effects*. That would exclude idealism (whether my version of it, which I have called dualism, or the version I do not believe, that claims *everything* is merely an idea, even matter).

MARX: Your second interpretation is correct.

SOCRATES: But this must require some very deep intuition, indeed, to comprehend. For I cannot comprehend how the laws of arithmetic change in a man's mind when his economy changes from a barter system, under feudalism, to a money system, under Capitalism, or from Capitalism to Communism. Whether he is counting sheep or coins or the heads of his bourgeois enemies, two plus three will always be five.

MARX: I am talking about ideological ideas, not mathematics. Your ideology changes with your class system.

SOCRATES: Of course it does! For a class system *is* an ideology. But you say that your religion and philosophy change too, don't you?

MARX: Yes. Read my next sentence.

SOCRATES: **"What else does the history of ideas prove, than that intellectual production changes in character in proportion as material production is changed?"**

Frankly, I think the history of ideas proves almost anything *but* that. Do you really mean to say that when my factories change from relying on water wheels to electrical dynamos, my mind changes from slow and watery to spark-filled and electrical? Isn't it almost the opposite? Didn't the mind first change and get smart and so invent electrical power and then make a material copy of what it invented?

And that strange phrase of yours—**"intellectual production"**—do you really think the mind is a kind of factory or assembly line for producing ideas?

MARX: La Mettrie proved that the mind was a machine. So did Hobbes.

SOCRATES: They asserted it. They did not prove it.

MARX: But read the next sentence.

SOCRATES: **"The ruling ideas of each age have ever been the ideas of its ruling class."**

MARX: *That* is what I mean by my previous sentence. You certainly can't deny *that*.

SOCRATES: Are you using your "snow job" trick again? There is nothing that you have said that I could more easily deny.

MARX: Now it is you who are using the "snow job".

SOCRATES: Not at all. Let's list the seven most influential thinkers of all time, whether they are right or wrong, good or bad, true or false. I would count them as follows: Jesus, myself, Buddha, Muhammad, Confucius, Moses, and you.

MARX: You put yourself second to Jesus?

SOCRATES: In influence, not in worth. No false modesty is able to survive here. I was the father of philosophy, and philosophy was the mother of the sciences, and science is the religion of modernity. I was the first to know how to argue logically.

MARX: All right, all right, I'm seventh, anyway.

SOCRATES: The list is not infallible. The point is simply this: every one of these seven, including both of us, refutes your principle. We all came *not* from the ruling class of our societies. We all challenged the ruling class. We were all feared by the ruling class. All the most influential people in history were nonconformists. Nothing could be farther from the truth than to say that we are all determined by our society in all that we think. What a conservative, status-quo philosophy that is for a self-styled radical like you!

MARX: I answer your calumny in my next paragraphs.

SOCRATES: I will read them and see.

When people speak of ideas that revolutionize society, they do but express the fact, that within the old society, the elements of a new one have been created, and that the dissolution of the old ideas keeps even pace with the dissolution of the old conditions of existence.

When the ancient world was in its last throes, the ancient religions were overcome

by Christianity. When Christian ideas suc-
cumbed in the eighteenth century to ratio-
nalist ideas, feudal society fought its death
battle with the then revolutionary bourgeoisie. The ideas of religious liberty and
freedom of conscience, merely gave expres-
sion to the sway of free competition within
the domain of knowledge.

Here, once again, is your foundational idea, your fundamental assumption: that thoughts are mere echoes
of the falling of coins; that freedom of mind or conscience is nothing but the echo in the mind of free
trade in the market. If this is so, then before the ad-
vent of Capitalism there was no such thing as freedom of conscience or mind, either in thought or in
reality. But abundant texts from pre-Capitalist societies simply and literally refute you, by data, not argument.

MARX: That is the objection that my next paragraphs
answer.

SOCRATES: Then to those we now turn.

MARX: I first formulate the objection:

"Undoubtedly," it will be said, "religious,
moral, philosophical and juridical ideas have
been modified in the course of historical development. But religion, morality, philosophy, political science, and law, constantly sur-
vived this change. There are, besides, eternal
truths, such as Freedom, Justice, etc., that are
common to all states of society. But Communism abolishes eternal truths, it abolishes

all religion and all morality, instead of con-
stituting them on a new basis; it therefore
acts in contradiction to all past historical experience."

And then I answer it:

What does this accusation reduce itself to?
The history of all past society has consisted
in the development of class antagonisms, antagonisms that assumed different forms at
different epochs. But whatever form they
may have taken, one fact is common to all
past ages, viz., the exploitation of one part
of society by the other. No wonder, then, that
the social consciousness of past ages, despite
all the multiplicity and variety it displays,
moves within certain common forms, or general ideas, which cannot completely vanish
except with the total disappearance of class
antagonisms.

The Communist revolution is the most
radical rupture with traditional property relations; no wonder that its development in-
volves the most radical rupture with traditional ideas.

SOCRATES: Is that your answer to the objection?

MARX: Yes.

SOCRATES: But it is not an answer to the objection at
all, even as you yourself formulated the objection. All
you did was to repeat the idea that was objected to.

MARX: In a popular pamphlet, my concern is not to prove every point by syllogistic logic, but clearly to assert the truth and to contrast it with prevailing error.

SOCRATES: So the "truth" you assert here is that there is nothing universal to humanity throughout history, nothing innate to human nature, no definition of man as such, as distinct from Communist man or Capitalist man or feudal man or classical man or Christian man or modern man—except one: man is the exploiter, the robber, the slaver. **"One fact is common to all past ages . . . exploitation."**

MARX: That is what I say.

SOCRATES: What an astonishingly dark philosophy! All unselfishness, all affection, all friendship, all sanctity, all self-sacrifice, all mother-love, all honor, all martyrdoms throughout history—all this is nothing but exploitation! The idea is so astonishing that it leaves me speechless and unable to refute it—like claiming that all living things on earth are really vampire bats in disguise, or that the number eight is really the number two, but our minds cannot recognize this.

And your other foundational assumption, that all ideas are nothing but the puppets of the puppet-master that is economics; that God and Freedom and Immortality and Truth and Goodness and Beauty and Justice and Wisdom and Love and Holiness are all nothing but shadows cast on the walls of our consciousness by the real actors in the human drama, which are coins!

MARX: Don't be so polite, Socrates; tell me what you really think of my philosophy. See, I, too, can be sarcastic.

SOCRATES: There is no hiding here, so I will tell you. I think these two ideas of yours are so utterly absurd, so logically self-contradictory, and also so insulting and demeaning to humanity, that they could have proceeded only from the mind of a great man-hater and self-hater, from a spiritual death wish, from a philosophy whose fundamental principle, as you quote from *Faust*, is that "everything that exists deserves to perish." I have examined thousands of philosophies over thousands of years, and I have seldom if ever found a single one as destructive as yours. Thrasymachus and Machiavelli were only tyrants; you are a terrorist.

MARX: Why, thank you, Socrates. You are a great flatterer!

21

The Steps to Communism

MARX: Do you really expect me to hang around and do polite logical dialogue with you after *that*?

SOCRATES: You have no choice. Neither do I. Our task is not finished. We must explore three more questions: first, the strategy and the steps that will bring the world to your Communist world order, which you list next in your text; second, your "bottom line"; and third, the reasons for ignoring nearly everything in the last half of your book, which is so filled with petty and totally outdated details that its boredom becomes fascinating. A pile of mud a foot high is boring, but a pile of mud a mile high is fascinating.

MARX: I see you are still in your flattering mode.

SOCRATES: Like most tyrants with an enormous ego, you tell the world exactly what your strategy is for enslaving it, as a terrorist filled with self-confidence may announce where he will strike before he does: **"The first step in the revolution by the working class, is to raise the proletariat to the position of ruling class, to win the battle of democracy."** You thus provide your enemies with the means of thwarting your strategy in its very first step: at the ballot box.

Next, once it gains power, **"the proletariat will use its political supremacy to wrest, by degrees, all capital from the bourgeoisie, to centralize all instruments of production in the hands of the State, i.e., of the proletariat organized as the ruling class. . . . Of course, in the beginning, this cannot be effected except by means of despotic inroads on the rights of property."**

So you candidly admit that you will seize power by any means that serve your end: by **"forcible overthrow"** of all existing conditions wherever you can and by the slower methods of persuasion and propaganda in free democracies. Free men must be persuaded to sell their freedom and become slaves. But once you have the power, you will seize the money of the bourgeoisie by **"despotic"** means.

You then specify the ways you will do this: by changing laws in nations where you have won power, and by bloody revolution and war where you have lost.

Here are your ten steps to Communism. Many of them were instituted even in non-Communist nations after your time. In fact, most readers of this list of yours who live 150 years after your time will be very surprised at some of the items you specify as radical and Communist ideas, since they will have become so ordinary. You write:

These measures will of course be different in different countries.

Nevertheless, in the most advanced countries, the following will be pretty generally applicable:

1. Abolition of property in land and application of all rents of land to public purposes.
2. A heavy progressive or graduated income tax.
3. Abolition of all right of inheritance.
4. Confiscation of the property of all emigrants and rebels.
5. Centralization of credit in the hands of the State, by means of a national bank with State capital and an exclusive monopoly.
6. Centralization of the means of communication and transport in the hands of the State.
7. Extension of factories and instruments of production owned by the State. . . .
8. Equal liability of all to labour. Establishment of industrial armies, especially for agriculture.
9. . . . Gradual abolition of the distinction between town and country, by a more equitable distribution of population over the country.
10. Free education for all children in public schools.

One of your disciples, an Italian named Gramsci, was more prophetic than you were concerning priorities on this list. He put first what you put tenth and last: propaganda. In school this is called "education"; outside schools it is called "communications" and "media". He said that Marxism would not win on the battlefield or in the ballot box but in the classrooms.

So between yourself and Gramsci, you warn the world quite candidly where its battlefields will be. It is certainly not your fault if they ignore these clear warnings.

And now I shall conclude with two more friendly points.

MARX: Friendly points? Oh, I'm sure you will. And the sun will rise in the west, and triangles will have five sides.

SOCRATES: First, I will praise your rhetoric. Your concluding peroration really rings, you know.

MARX: I know.

SOCRATES: Even though not a single other revolution or party or leader paid the slightest attention to it in 1848, the "year of revolutions" throughout Europe.

MARX: I was too original for them.

SOCRATES: Your best phrases were all utterly unoriginal. In fact, they were plagiarisms. You stole **"the workers have no country"** from Marat, and also **"the proletarians have nothing to lose but their chains."** You stole **"religion is the opiate of the people"** from Heine, **"workers of all countries, unite!"** from Schapper, **"the dictatorship of the proletariat"** from Blanqui, and **"from each according to his abilities, to each according to his needs"** from Louis Blanc. You are a great propagandist only because you are a great thief.

MARX: It is the effects that count, not the causes. Whatever its source, great propaganda has great power to produce effects. It attracts.

SOCRATES: It does. But whom does propaganda attract? Who is the proper mate for a proper gander but a proper goose?

MARX: Since you are humiliating me with your "humor", will you at least grant me the justice of one last request?

SOCRATES: What is it?

MARX: May I have the last word and quote my own text's last words?

SOCRATES: You may quote yourself, but you may not have the last word. That privilege must be reserved for Another, who had also the first Word.

MARX: Let us hear the conclusion of all matters, the "bottom line".

The Communists disdain to conceal their views and aims. They openly declare that their ends can be attained only by the forcible overthrow of all existing social conditions. Let the ruling classes tremble at a Communistic revolution. The proletarians have nothing to lose but their chains. They have a world to win. WORKING MEN OF ALL COUNTRIES, UNITE!

SOCRATES: Those words were destined, indeed, to fall like a match to incinerate your world. There are billions of souls and millions of bodies who will confront you in this world with their burns. If you face here those wounds that you refused to face there, even you may find cleansing and light in the end.

MARX: And what do you have to do with this, Socrates?

SOCRATES: I shall continue to help you to "know thyself" even after this conversation ends.

MARX: How can you do that?

SOCRATES: Although you did not believe in the "I" or in prayer or in God or in your soul, I will pray that God will have mercy on your soul, though I have had no mercy on your book.

And now my second friendly point . . .

MARX: Oh, was that your first "friendly" point? I must have missed it.

SOCRATES: As I missed the sun rising in the west and triangles having five sides. My last friendly point is a piece of mercy. I will excuse us both: you for writing the rest of your book, chapters 3 and 4, and myself from reading it.

MARX: Why?

SOCRATES: Why, because it is such unendurably dull and petty stuff—all little local details that became quickly outdated.

MARX: Outdated! Why?

SOCRATES: Because it was so up-to-date. As a wise man once said, "He who marries the Spirit of the Times will very soon become a widower."

MARX: There are very important things in those chapters.

SOCRATES: No, there are not. You always had a fantastically exaggerated view of little things and a fantastically diminished view of great things. You thought the sun and the moon rose and set in your lap.

MARX: This is your "friendly" point?

SOCRATES: No. The friendly point is that I wanted to excuse you for writing it. You wrote it hurriedly under the pressure of your publisher's deadline.

MARX: That is so.

SOCRATES: Because, as usual, you had spent all the money you had. And almost all of it was not earned, but was gifts or loans that you rarely paid back. You were a continual and disastrous failure at managing time and money. Only one who was such a failure at personal economics could possibly have worshipped economics as you did; and only one who could not manage time could possibly have worshipped the goddess History, whom your ancestors reviled as "the strumpet Fortune".

MARX: Oh, thank you for being so "friendly".

SOCRATES: You also were, quite simply and literally, a liar.

MARX: Prove it! By specifics and by data, please, from my public writings.

SOCRATES: That is so easy that a child could do it. What about that famous and influential quotation from Gladstone that you deliberately misquoted and twisted to say exactly the opposite of what it did say? You insisted on putting it in every edition of *Capital*, and you refused to correct it or omit it even after it was exposed and refuted. You defended it with infinite oceans of obfuscation all the rest of your life. You also deliberately changed Adam Smith's words and meaning when you quoted him. And you called yourself a *scientist*?

You also despised the actual proletariat yet called yourself a proletarian. You and all your friends came from the well-to-do middle class, the bourgeoisie; yet you fulminated against everything bourgeois as against Hell itself. "Bourgeois" was your most venomous and ubiquitous curse word.

You claimed to pity the poor factory workers and claimed to be the expert who alone could help them; yet you never once in your life set foot in a factory.

You exalted work and railed against idleness; yet you never worked, except to write. You were idle and despised the only relative you had who was hardworking, successful, and knowledgeable about conditions under Capitalism, your uncle Lion Philips, founder of the Philips Electric Company. You were most hostile to your revolutionary friends who did have some work experience. You hated the calm and disciplined skilled workers you met in London and Germany: they were too reasonable, too realistic, too practical for your visions of doom and destruction. When you founded the Communist League, you eliminated all working-class members, for you were, quite simply, a snob.

You were absolutely merciless and venomous against anyone who preferred peace to war, moderation to extremism, or incremental steps to sudden violence—Weitling, for instance. You were, quite simply, a thoroughgoing and consummate hypocrite.

MARX: What if I was? My individual character does not matter. I was history's instrument to accomplish great things. I cannot dispute any of the things you say, because of the terrible truth-telling character of this place. But I call on you to tell the whole truth not only about me but about Communism—not in ideology or morality or any mere idea, which you have tried to do in our arguments, but in history, which is fact. You have dropped hints and scattered details of your knowledge of the history of my world after my death; give us the whole truth, please.

SOCRATES: I am very happy you ask, and I am very happy to answer. Here is what history made of your philosophy—no, I will not use that precious word, for it means "the love of wisdom"—here is what history made of your ideology.

Bourgeois Capitalism did not die or weaken. It grew in size, in popularity, and in its ability to satisfy mankind's needs. It grew continually, with only a few setbacks and interruptions and depressions. By the turn of the millennium, 150 years after you, it was the only successful economic system on earth, with no signs of decay or revolution. In fact, people liked it; it made more people more prosperous and more content than any alternative.

On the other hand, socialism and Communism were spectacular economic failures nearly everywhere. Communism rose to power only by lies, assassinations, and terror. It ruled half the world for most of the twentieth century. And then it simply died. Not a drop of blood was spilled; it died simply because after seventy years of it, no one wanted it any more or believed it any more.

It did not free the proletariat but enslaved them, both economically and politically. Whole peoples were massacred. Well over a hundred million people were killed in its name. One Communist dictator, in China, killed fifty million political enemies. Another, in Cambodia, murdered one-third of all his country's people. Another, in Russia, engineered mass starvation of millions and set up an enormous network throughout his nation of secret police and concentration camps. Everywhere Communism took power, it ruled by terror. Your ideology is directly responsible for the most enormous suffering, bloodshed, and tyranny in the history of the world.

Your politics stemmed from the French Revolution, especially its all-or-nothing fanaticism and its use of sheer terror. Your disciples instituted the Jacobins' Reign of Terror on a worldwide scale for three generations.

A man whose soul and face and movements eerily resembled yours came to power in Germany largely because the German people so feared and hated Communism that they turned to this man, who promised to destroy it. His system was called "*National* Socialism", but its likenesses to yours far outweighed its differences. He nearly destroyed the world. He was probably the most hated man in history.

If you had attained the power you desired, you might have surpassed him. But the strange mercies of divine providence gave you the undeserved gift of weakness and failure and thus spared you and gave you some little hope, which still remains.

MARX: I am appalled.

SOCRATES: Therein is your hope.

MARX: I simply do not know what to say.

SOCRATES: And there is a second reason for hope. You are learning Lesson One: to know your own ignorance.

MARX: In other words, I am beginning to sound like you.

SOCRATES: A little while ago you tried to persuade me to think like you and to join your ideology and your party. It was impossible, of course, because we have no ideologies or parties here. But you must join *me*—not in ideology, for I have none, but in my mission, which never ends: to know the one thing you avoided most, your self.

MARX: Am I in Hell?

SOCRATES: You are in yourself, forever. Whether that is Heaven or Hell is up to you.

MARX: I have a choice, then?

SOCRATES: On earth you had the choice each moment to open or close your eyes to the truth. No oppression or prison could remove that freedom. Here, you no longer have that choice; here, no eye can close. The only choices here are the ones we made on earth, but now seen with total clarity and confronted. That seeing is the purgatorial process you have begun with me. But even there, in the first world, you had no freedom really to escape yourself, only your self-consciousness. The eye remains even when it closes. For there really is a self, and you yourself are the one person you can never escape, in life or in death.

MARX: Am I in an eternal prison, then? Will I never have my freedom?

SOCRATES: You will never have the freedom that everyone else who ever lived has had: the freedom from being Karl Marx.

Acknowledgment

Karl Marx and Friedrich Engels, *The Communist Manifesto*, translated by Samuel Moore (London: Penguin Books, 1967, reprinted 1985). All quotes from Marx (in bold type) that are not otherwise identified were taken from this title.